EDITORIAL

FIONA SAMPSON

If "the poetry of place" is one of those old-fashioned, ambiguous phrases we love to hate, why use it? Does it really mean "places" are "poetic"? In any case, what *isn't* a place? Doesn't everywhere have to be *somewhere* – isn't everywhere some kind of place? Nor am I clear, despite a couple of decades spent grappling with verse itself, what metaphorical or synaesthetic magic allows us to say the actual trees and streets we live among are "poetry".

Of course, "the poetry of place" does also mean poems coming from places: in Britain, our thoughts turn immediately to the Romantic tradition of landscape "shock and awe". To be honest, I'm more attracted by notions of belonging. Just liking something doesn't necessarily give me anything interesting to say about it; but coming from somewhere – a setting or a culture – must leave me with a fuller than usual understanding of that place. Unless we're only interested in verse as pattern-making we do, after all, like poems to offer insights. Maybe this is why poetry which is aware of its own cultural baggage can be so fascinating.

"Place" isn't just elsewhere, of course. It can also be *here*. While this issue of *PR* is joyously international, it also celebrates British poets "going local". At the heart of this movement in British poetry since the 1990s is our lead essayist. Sean O'Brien's 'Journey to the Interior', one of his Newcastle Lectures, looks at the construction of local, non-metropolitan 'Ideas of England': which must steer round the twin traps of post-Betjeman twee-ness and shaven-headed primitivism. Poets putting this into practice in this issue include Sarah Corbett, Sharon Morris and even, perhaps, Robin Robertson's haunted Scot abroad in the Great Wen.

Understanding that international verse has some of the same ambivalence about simply rehearsing where it's from is key to valuing it. Some of the most exciting writing in this issue comes from places which aren't far away as the plane flies, but whose traditions are far indeed from Anglo-Saxon poetry. Here, with a burst of Mediterranean charisma, Palestine, the Lebanon and Greece rub shoulders thanks to their translator-advocates Fady Joudah, Socrates Kabouropoulos and Omar Sabbagh. Elsewhere, we include poetry by Portugal's Casimiro de Brito, C.K. Stead writing from New Zealand, Yang Lian's fine collaboration with Pascale Petit, and another installment of Marilyn Hacker's valuable 'Porte Ouverte on the Francophonie'. Doesn't so much richness and colour just make you want to book a summer holiday – whether at home or abroad?

CONTRIBUTORS

Louis Bourne is Professor of Spanish at Georgia College & State University, USA, and has published many translations of contemporary Spanish poetry. **Casimiro de Brito**'s latest collection, published 2011, is *Amar a Vida Inteira* (*Loving the Whole of Life*). **Claire Crowther**'s *Incense* has just been published by Flarestack Poets. **Menna Elfyn**'s bilingual collection, *Murmur*, is published in September by Bloodaxe. **Diane Fahey**'s *The Wing Collection: New & Selected Poems* was published by Puncher and Wattmann in 2011. **John Greening**'s *To the War Poets* is due from OxfordPoets in 2013. **Vona Groarke**'s most recent collection, *Spindrift* (Gallery Press), was a PBS Recommendation. **Marilyn Hacker** is the author of twelve books of poems, including *Names* (Norton, 2009) and *Essays on Departure* (Carcanet Press, 2006). **Fady Joudah**'s second collection, *Alight*, is due from Copper Canyon Press in 2013. **Vénus Khoury-Ghata** is a Lebanese poet and novelist; her lastest collection is *Où vont les arbres* (Mercure de France, 2011). **Yang Lian**'s latest collection in English translation is *Lee Valley Poems* (Bloodaxe, 2009). **Erik Martiny** is the editor of *A Companion to Poetic Genre* for Wiley-Blackwell. **Karen McCarthy Woolf** was a runner up in the Cardiff International Poetry Prize 2011 and is published in *Ten New Poets* (Bloodaxe 2010). **Kim Moore** won an Eric Gregory Award and the Geoffrey Dearmer Prize in 2011. **Sharon Morris**'s second collection *Gospel Oak* (Enitharmon Press) will be published in December. **Jeri Onitskansky** is a poet and Jungian analyst in private practice in London. **Pascale Petit**'s *What the Water Gave Me: Poems after Frida Kahlo* (Seren, 2010) was shortlisted for the T.S. Eliot Prize and Wales Book of the Year. **Ian Pindar**'s *Constellations* is forthcoming from Carcanet. **Christopher Reid**'s *Selected Poems* has just been published by Faber. **Robin Robertson**'s fifth collection will be published in 2013. **Anthony Rudolf** is a poet and solo translator, mainly from French and Russian, and co-translates from the Hebrew with **Miriam Neiger-Fleischmann**, who is a painter as well as a poet. **Omar Sabbagh**'s second collection, *The Square Root of Beirut* (Cinnamon Press) has just been published. **Tomaž Šalamun**'s *On the Tracks of Wild Game* is published shortly by Ugly Duckling Presse. **John Siddique**'s latest collection is *Full Blood* (Salt). **Kathryn Simmonds** is the author of *Sunday at the Skin Launderette* (Seren). **Catherine Smith**'s next collection, *Otherwhere*, is forthcoming from Smith/Doorstop in 2012. **Martha Sprackland** was twice a Foyle Young Poet and is editor of *Cake* magazine. **Anne Stevenson**'s new collection, *Astonishment*, is forthcoming from Bloodaxe. **Alan Stubbs** is an Arvon prizewinner and was shortlisted for the Bridport prize. **Michael Thomas Taren**'s book *Motherhood* was a 2010 finalist for the Fence Poetry Series. **Anthony Thwaite**'s *Late Poems* (Enitharmon) was published in 2010. He edited Philip Larkin's *Letters to Monica* (Faber, 2010). **Ben Wilkinson**'s pamphlet of poems is *The Sparks* (Tall Lighthouse, 2008). **Valerie Wohlfeld**'s *Woman with Wing Removed* was published by Truman State University Press, 2010. **Ghassan Zaqtan** is a prominent Palestinian poet; a translation selection by Fady Joudah, *Like a Straw Bird It Follows Me*, is available from Yale University Press.

L C K Head

Contents

Volume 102:1 Spring 2012

Editorial

Poems

[handwritten margin notes:]
- List poets title + poems
- see Kathleen Jamie's Prose/poetry (recent)
- see Lunch under Gonf
- see Dorkington festival
- see Ledbury.

Centrefold

The National Poetry Competition

Reviews

POEMS

The moon eats her heart out again and again
But the rivers just go with the flow, my dear...

– Kathryn Simmonds

Robin Robertson
Falconer's Farewell

She kept a cast of merlins
mewed in her own chamber; let him
fletch his shafts with each new
throw of feathers.

He strung his bow with sinew, so he'd draw
on the very nerve of a deer, and he loosed
with such speed and gift
he could pin a pair of arrows
on the head of a man, like horns.

When she heard the lark ringing up high
over September, she slipped herself free;
her blue hunger reading the sky – the land
already running under her.

His flights missed their mark, slid
on the hard, dry ground, snaked
into the grass. When he looked for them
he felt them, snapping underfoot. And her,
his falconer, nowhere to be found.

A Visit

I was walking through her garden
dead-heading the dried-out stalks,
the faded, stiff remains
of the neighbours' cats,
each one pinned with pine needles
like a punctured Christ.

I passed the tree in flames
hearing the sound of a sword in the air,
the sound of a sword
being drawn from a sheath.
She waits beyond all this
as the glove waits for the hand

till I lower myself onto her, the witch,
burrowing under her clothes
for the breasts: the nipples
nesting in the black, wiry hairs
where I can nose
and suckle.

Interesting

Fugitive In London

I use these streets to disappear;
thirty years of ducking round corners
to throw them off the scent,

losing myself in crowds, diving
underground and coming up
like a cormorant, miles downstream.

Night after night, the same dream
of having murdered someone,
hidden them under the floor.

It got so bad I lifted the boards
to look, to see what I'd done. The boy
I'd killed and buried there was me.

Ghassan Zaqtan
Neighbouring Sounds

Yesterday I became aware of some cheerful steps
before I heard a "besmala"
whose dust was weeping.

I had just seen a woman
who was alight for a moment and then vanished...
but her coat lingered in the shadows.

I heard a music from the neighbouring basement,
a string instrument falling and withering,
and a wrecked laugh that had arrived from the tunnels
under the house, a laugh whose yarn
time surrounds and whose swerve
is led by some damp metal.

And I saw in what the blind see
a sound in the garden,
its form
and breath,
before I woke up alone...
some murmur sprang from the walls
and resembled the air
as it says to you: Here... here

or the air saying to you: Here
                              here

Who's in the city besides us?

Not Yet

Whenever I say it's time I went
and got ready to leave
all the faces I nearly forgot
call to me and the houses
I stayed at and leaned
my head against their brick
or corridor walls come...
and out of their waters
where to the end of endlessness
the rooms crawl I am called.

Whenever I say it's time I went
the songs I thought would never return arrive
and the old hands knock on my door
hands that thought of me
or shepherded my roads
in a time that was... obliterated.

The same hands that cuffed my wrists
and gripped my collar
and woke me from sleep...
dead
      and living
at the door O my master
O Mohammad!

The Bird Follows Me

In the year two thousand or a little before, there might have been
a prelude that inhabited me, it resembled summer
in the rooms of bachelors,
I used to spin it in my speech...

Like a pleasant gait on an edge of marble, or dusting it
from what the hoofs of mules leave behind
as they climb the wadi

"...in my house
women give birth to rings
and disappear from the world beyond the door,
here's the paradise of the one I love
and the journey
of the one who saw..."

A prelude like other preludes
I didn't retrieve from muttering

Like a straw bird
it follows me…

Translated by Fady Joudah

TEXTU POEMS

Fady Joudah
Iron Maiden

We're in the no reply zone
still I will bang my body

into your body's rhythms
We know god is OK with it

touching jamming
silence with our breaths

The Chosen

There's no ram inside me
to offer to a place

Every morning is imaginary
& every people is invented

A woman kissed is not a woman
in a kiss kissing

Eurydice

Low visibility midsummer fog
you are deaf cold your eyes

a grasshopper statute
of limitations on return

Now you are declassified
it is about to snow

Honey Comb

Wisdom comes late
a pomegranate's caviar womb

Penicillin kills what kills what kills
a cat chases its tail

and an infant
tracks shadow like a wolf

Divorce

Persephone your yearly sabbatical
was always brief and forced

You couldn't begin or end a book
but wrote

"Not Catholic and more
stunning than Azrael"

The Textu Poem
The 'u' in textu might echo the one in haiku, but it also emphasises the intimate or private
'you' in dialogue. A Textu poem has only one hard rule: that it be exactly 160 characters long,
specific to text-message space, size and definition. Theme, form and style are unrestricted.
Perhaps the Textu form also offers us a poem in which metre is defined by character
count, not syllable.

Claire Crowther
Ad Astra

So strongwilled, the thumb of sun
                                    on sea,
that its aquamarine flashes
like a poor contact. Eye-stinging flash, on off on.
Something dazzling has been wrong
                                    with me:

I've climbed through life looking up.
                                    These doors
grip the street's staircase as I do.
I'm shaded by further heights of terrace. Soft toys
lie on roof tiles below me –
                                    old lures.

The village has seen collapse
                                    in land-
slide and flood. Fishermen have drowned
in the bay, and poets. They're cold metal, these rails,
hardly warmed by the sweat of
                                    my hand.

Reaching the starry bushes,
                                    capers
springing from the ruined castle walls,
softening them as figs ripen on local thorns,
a rumpled packaging of
                                    lost wars,

having picked off some small fruits –
                                    I think
at last, 'Look down.' So does the sun:
electromagnetic solar waves are startling
sea waves to swink blank swink blank
                                    swink blank.

A.J. Stubbs

the slight curved feather saved from the fallen
tucked in between the print of a painting of an unknown
woman, against the wall, is softly held and pliable
all of its ribs shiver as it peeps from her gathered-up hair
the wells of her eyes look out the infinite, and suffer
smoulderingly blurry as twin black holes above a
blunted nose that divides an oily yellow-fleshed moon
down to the chasm of a mouth that also seems prim
is also waiting somehow, the parted lips are bruised
on rather than brushed in to the thick mastic paint
layered on, and worked on, again, and this feather is
much too frivolous to be here where there are no whispered
accusations hiding in the corners, and her aching breasts
are covered and shielded from all of the naked silences

Tomaž Šalamun
Great-great-grandfathers

Why did I draw a line?
the line can:
be touched with hands
you can put a tree on it
you can wet it
you can lie on it
you can shut your eyes, to not see it
you can go for a walk on it
with your son in a gallery
you can step on one part of it
with your right leg, you can step on
another part of it with your left leg
and say: from here
to here
you can pack earth onto it
and eat wheat
you can realize there is no bran
you can say, every rhomb is made
of a line
you can shout across a gallery:
Tinkara, where are you? and
Tinkara in the gallery shouts back:
I'm pasturing sheep, I'm pasturing sheep
so the sound waves touch the line.

The line cannot be:
used as a spice
for food
has no attributes
and is without crevasses
you cannot make her
creak

if you poke it into the earth
to make it sprout, it won't sprout
it is without a sense of before
noon or afternoon
it does not contain fluoride
it has no logos tied up around
its waist
it has no logos tied up around its neck
it has no coil and it
does not drip
honey
you cannot mistake it for
Erwin Panowsky
you cannot walk her on the edge
of a bridge.

The relation between you can and you cannot
is art,
therefore the line is art.

I stood on ice.
My mother went to the market with
a basket full of flowers to sell it
to the rich ones.
She didn't sell it.
I turned my palm.
Enough for the storm to pull down the beams
hewed by my grandfather
And my mother still has
a young, lean body
pleasing to horses and peasants.

Translated by Michael Thomas Taren and the author

Valerie Wohlfeld
My Hair, My Heart

Once my hair was light and my heart was dark—
I did not know the workings of the heart
or how blood ebbs and flows like a seamark
in wet sand. Light hair is no counterpart

to the dim mechanisms of the pulse—
they are two quite different things,
one is a compulsion for the sun and one is a convulsion
in the valve, a little shudder in the hinge

that swings open, shut. Then suddenly
the strands of hair that filled my brush were not bright,
and in the tall glass mirror I could see
my hair was dark and my heart was light.

My heart was light, the hidden blood beat—
but my hair, my hair was dark as the waters of Lethe.

Marilyn Hacker
Sapphics In Winter

Rain falls till and through the five-thirty nightfall
as this time I walk with you to the métro,
going different places, of course, but on the
same rush-hour subway.

Winter trees and scarves over quilted jackets,
folded headlines cover the small disasters.
Three days' massacres trump a decade's failures,
linked though they might be.

You are young and what I began to tell you
was the wrought-iron grille of a conversation,
curlicues, non-sequiturs, screens unfolded
hiding a rag-heap.

You're already elsewhere, redeemed from exile,
blue-green eyes assessing the slack and blemish
as I kiss you back to the intifada –
kissed at a distance.

Porte Ouverte On The Francophonie: *Marilyn Hacker*

Vénus Khoury-Ghata
Four Poems

The stale bread on the windowsill fed the ants and the angel of the house
his feathers on the rainy pane protected us from the spite
of the linden tree, true owner of the grounds
Our fingers drew him standing to the right of the god of repentance
                                      and frugality

shoulders unsteady as a scale at the end of market day

God of abundance and of friendly locusts
who cracks walnuts with the back of your hand
polish the mother's pots with the sun you keep in your pocket
fill them with your bees' buzzing
put a ring on every one of our pigeons' fingers.

The armies of dust raised by her broom ate the door our notebooks
                              and her necklace
belched up bits of pearl
It was war
The bloody battles between those who chewed on our first-communion
      smiles and those who lapped up the salt from the kitchen sink went
                            on beneath the mother's skirt
in the dark at the bottom of her well

Bare-chested
the cemetery guard couldn't care less about the sun that hunted down
                                                                    the steles
the snails gathered from the cracks in the marble will finish on dinner
                                                                    plates
stuffed with garlic and confusion
They contain the thoughts of souls captured without their knowing it
Souls, they say, put their grievances out on the tablecloth and
eat their fill of the chime of knives on porcelain

Ragged plane-tree harder to drive away than a beggar in front of the
                                                                    church on Sunday
That became a door
That became a double-doored coffin
We preferred the monastery's linden with its pockets filled with squirrels
The pilgrims who tied their mules to its trunk drank the saint's water
and the mother's upright without stopping
When night had been chased away with torch-flares
the mother sang turtledoves to us
sang us torrential rains
to wipe away our disgrace
and age us

Translated by Marilyn Hacker

Anthony Thwaite

i.m. Peter Reading, 1946-2011

Despair; desuetude; drink –
Not a bad trio
To celebrate in concert

One who hammered out music
Percussive, classic,
Whatever's left of something

Plangent, bereft, and bankrupt:
The dying planet
Drifting down to daft giggles.

Jeri Onitskansky
There Is No Elsewhere

Snow falls through the mist onto fallen snow,
erasing all but the colour of leaping
made by the dozen or so horses I just barely make out
as a colt takes the apple from my palm in one bite
and searches the snow for fallen chunks.
Even the men hauling carrots in burlap sacks
are a raging flurry, puffing down the lane
their lorry got stuck in, wheels frozen sundials.
But perspective's blown and the sun is lost
in mist that is inseparable from the field it swallows.
In the blinding, there is no elsewhere –
clouds ice the lips of my boots and distance
banks in the timelessness of trees. As earlier
in the day, my mind drifted in our talk – like mist,
like storm – and I worried that I'd gone.
Until I remembered: wandering makes me here
distinctly. My thoughts floated like snowflakes cut out
from your own illustrious pages; catching
humorously in the cedar, blurring sadly in the holly.

Anne Stevenson
Demeter And Her Daughter

Demeter speaks:

Just at the worst time, May!
I was teaching my ignorant soils
How to manage the flowers,
So was looking another way
When the silly girl tripped on the coils
Of ophidian Nether Powers,
And the bastard bore her away.

In my fury in June and July,
I punished the grass.
I wrung the clouds dry of their rain
And let the flowers die.
I ordered the sun as he passed
To burn the collaborative grain;
Then I stormed him out of the sky!

Well, he told me where she had gone,
Even cannoned a shaft for me –
A filthy hole – to the land
Where tubers and roots are born.
And there sat Persephone
With that criminal hand in hand
On a mound of dung like a throne.

"Is that you, mother?" she cried,
"Fuck off! Don't bother me here,
This is *my* space!
Can't you be satisfied
Bossing two thirds of the year
From your own high place
Without grafting me to your side?"

"You watch your language," I said,
Controlling myself. The foul air
Stank of bitumen,
It was damp as a urinal there.
When I saw that my child had died
While not yet fully a woman,
I broke down and cried.

How do you think they responded?
They laughed! They fancied a joint!
They pointedly smoked *my* weed
Entwined on their dungy bed –
Until, in astonishment,
They watched every tear I shed
Become a seed, each seed

Branch into a stem,
Dicotyledon at first
But in seconds a creeping bramble,
Beneath, before, behind them,
As a desert becomes a jungle
After a cloudburst.
I told that miracle to bind them,

Forgetting the offending oaf
Hades, as he used to be,
Or Pluto – pick your nomenclature –
Was also a god, my brother
Who splits my heritage with me.
There in the bowels of the earth
He held the hegemony.

So my thorny lianas weakened
In that tunnelled air.
Starved of celestial energy,
· They peaked and sickened,
Flopped back like filthy hair –
Now worms, now whips, now graffiti,
Now *son et lumière*.

Then mud hot as hangover sweat
Oozed out of a cave
Composted with glittering slime.
The place was a communal grave
Where Death, in his element,
Stirs into compact time,
My hideous nourishment.

Oh, how had my beautiful darling –
Under age, anorexic, depressed –
Become his queen?
Now listen, because in the telling
This story – a myth at best –
At its tabloid worst has been
Skewed by corrupt reporting.

I insist that the truth be told.
Hades grows no fruit.
That over-sold pomegranate
Was indigestible gold.
Persephone never touched it.
All she ate was one shrivelled
Loganberry, grey with mould.

But it tasted of my tears.
So she upped stakes and came to me
In a sort of daze.
Maybe for the first time in years,
She considered her ways.
Maybe she was hungry
Or needed to wash her clothes.

Whatever it was, she chose
To walk out on her lover
Without a word of apology.
Their affair, it seems, was over,
Though, knowing how the world goes,
I supposed the split was temporary.
Thank goodness, it was.

For once Persephone was home,
She couldn't live a day with me
Without a quarrel.
Spring came, grain grew, sun shone,
Buds flowered. She hated us all.
At last, dying to be alone,
I set her free.

When, one rainy day in October,
She was gone, I was almost glad.
She did nothing but smoke,
Mope and be rude
When I tried to talk to her.
I love her. I knew she'd come back.
As she still does, summer after summer.

Ye unjust gods, I've tried!
I can't get through to her.
I've always been faithful and dignified,
And she's – well, a slut.
Everything ugly appeals to her,
She loves her muck.
The future is hers to decide.

John Greening
American Music

Samuel Barber asked for croutons to be scattered at his funeral.
From the cortege, as the fresh soil steamed, adagio,
Feldman, Carter, Crumb and all the products of Boulanger
approached to salute and pepper him with their hard pieces.

Catherine Smith
The Lip Stitcher

I come with my little bag
            – needles and gauze,
cat-gut and scissors.

Every lip's
            a cushion, a jelly-fish
full of nerve-endings.
            Every stab is agony.
Blood pools,
            blackens like warm tar.

I have stitched the lips
            of lovers who fear they'll
cry out in their sleep;
            the lips of asylum seekers
in filthy, blistering
            detention camps
and on the steps of cold
            stone altars
in English churches.

I have stitched the lips
            of Bolivian prostitutes
who swore they'd starve
            if the brothels closed,
if they couldn't fill
            their mouths with
their regulars' cocks.

I have stitched the lips
              of blasphemers and Saints
and those who crave
              the pain of the needle –
who winced
              but wanted more
in basements
              in Hackney
and Birmingham.

I have stitched the lips
              of the dead,
so the soul stays put,
              and won't cry out.

I come with my little bag
              – needles and gauze,
cat-gut and scissors.

Kim Moore
Those Things We Did

in that bed-length room, with bare brick
on every wall, and the thumping of the club
across the road, that Sunday lunchtime rave
with the boys in pink and green and yellow
and your head on my pillow like a pocketful
of change, and students walking up and down
the hallway, and six televisions blaring,
and playing Dylan as if we'd discovered him,
the wall crumbling under my open palm,
the fire alarm that cried for three nights
in a row, and we ignored it, while our friends
gathered outside in pyjamas and played football,
we stayed naked and stupid with each other,
went on to do terrible things to one another.

temporarily deposited?

Christopher Reid
The Cry

The child woke to a cry, not his.
It came from beyond: a cry
of the absolute night. But it wasn't
a ghost. It wasn't a beast.
It wasn't a truck or a train. It was
a closer cry, of something like pain,
deep-fetched, both pushing and dragging,
torn, with its long-straggling, humanoid roots
protesting, from a soil that clogged and clung
and was reluctant to let it be born,
breathe air, take flight.
Perhaps some, even most, of the cry
agreed, with a lullaby croon
or wheedle, preferring to sleep,
or to die. But the rest of the cry
had put up a fight against itself:
an urgent, delirious skirmish.
Which it must win. Which it did,
with a short-lasting whimper
of triumph and release.
In the peace that followed,
the child lay awake, unable to explain
why he was stirred by a thing
so ugly, so sad and so frightening;
nor why he wanted to hear it again.

The Coin

(interesting)

Being dead, I was ready for
the journey. They put a coin,
one obol, the standard fare,
under my tongue – now still,
but not yet cold.
I had not been told
that this would happen.
But a shut mouth is, I thought,
as safe a purse as any.
The taste, which would have made me
wince and scowl before,
and spit the nasty thing out,
was neither here nor there.
So I took my pill without a fuss,
and set off like a child
walking for the first time
to catch the morning bus,
under a sky both bright
and hazy, fraught
with promise of adventure.
The world was just beginning,
there could be no end,
and the coin was my sole
possession, my secret friend.
So long as my lips kept tight,
what could go wrong?
Oh, I wish they had warned me
about the boatman who,
with his strong, hard fingers –
stinking of fish, or something –
prised my jaw open and withdrew
the mite, the token,
the less than a button,
that he claimed as his due.

Yang Lian
Questions About The Demon Taotie

The Pole Star is set in the centre of his forehead.
The deep blue   is crystalline   his ice pupil
has destroyed everything   Does the lonely
boiled girl embrace everything?

Escaping from Anyang   is an escape into the Yin night
No other light except this sight
luxuriously grinding a huge axe
Where did the tender broken limbs fall?

Looking up   for thousands of years
we sink down   Water always grinds its teeth
beneath us   the girl collapsing to a gurgle
Does Taotie seize   or chew?

Thousands of words re-split open are still
the one character   that one stroke captures life's flow
has been cooked ten thousand times   the flesh still soaked in sorrow
to reawaken   Is seizing   chewing?

This face is even more ruthless
than non-being   this powerlessness
staring out rams a hole
to pound away   What beauty is not bloody?

Our floating life is carved
on the shallow bronze relief   Does
the pupil's axle icily shrink space?
How many suns don't rise or set in the darkness of naming?

The girl swings gracefully back from the Yin
night   Does a thin fragrance snuff out all light?
Do bestial and human faces gently clasp vapour?
Has unutterable language   finally fulfilled the sacrifice?

Translated by Pascale Petit

C.K. Stead
The Afterlife

Jet lag's like
anaesthesia or
death. Early evening

it strikes, only to
resurrect you
at 2 a.m.

thinking of young
Alexander
Shelley conducting

Schumann, his
body a dancer's.
I tell the person

in my bed (who
proves to be you, my
darling) I feel

like lunch and a
nice game of tennis.
'Wrong season' she

murmurs forgetting
we haven't played
these forty years.

Unsure of the
map of my own
bedroom I travel

the world seeing
the fox in Queen's Park,
the giant fish

I named Carp Diem
in the millpond
at Gaiole,

and my New York
friend in a yellow
cab in a

line that stretches
all the way to
a dream of breakfast.

Of Course

My dying friend's face
was like paper or parchment,
his open mouth and long upper lip
trembling with each hard breath,
but as I was leaving
one eye came alive
as if he'd thought of something funny
and would tell me – later.

Out in the corridor when
I wished his wife good luck
I thought she blanched as if
I'd said that all her praying
(to the Virgin especially)
counted for nothing, and that
he'd have to take his chances
along with the rest.

not needed (I had of course.)

intensity style.

Ian Pindar ✓ (poet)

Sweetness, some cloudlessness, some shapes,
a random horse, the rolling arrangement
of the mind, with eyes open.

Fluttering gold limbs of brown leaves
sunned by straight cloudless blue in October,
bits and pieces of the sometimes Sunday.   ?

A real skyline for its own sake.
Not regret in the sky but late light,
little certainty in the dusk.

Old cars and roses. The yard prepares for evening.
It knows the colour of yesterday,
as the shapes in the yard are angles of themselves.

This night of royal blue can taste the sea,
reflected in a field of smoothness,
gulls tumbling over the tide.

The tide goes out, the tide comes in.
Everything seems to want to be
electric. Everything comes alive.

Sarah Wardle
Chinese Calligraphy

Music is the same character as happiness.
Upright is like, but not the same as, heaven,
which with some alteration turns to peace.

For some reason the past looks like yellow
while eternity is similar to source
and city reminiscent of purple.

A book seems related to the end.
Safe and dark could easily be confused.
Heart needs more strokes to make it forget.

John Greening
Field

Think of those artists who will never
escape the shadow of one they had
the bad luck to precede, who did

it first but not quite as stunningly
as the name we now remember. John
Field, for example, 'inventor of

the Nocturne', who nodded off while
Chopin opened the five-bar gate
and walked all over him.

Vona Groarke
How To Read A Building

Don't. You might as well say a morning convenes
in panelled reflections of itself. Or call the way
a roofline predicts its likely outcome, fate. Write 'arch',
and the word has to position itself between noun and
adjective. Put 'Lintel' as a title: see what comes of it.
I, too, may think of line endings with every quoin
or cant; of surface meaning caulked airtight;
of metaphor constructed as a tinted curtain wall.
I am alive, yes, to the notion of cantilevered sound,
open to rhymes between stone and stained glass,
sunlight and cement. Say what you like, but there's
a name for every kind of window you could possibly
see through. But the room with no window has
no first line and all its stowaway fictions need
to be written in dark ink. So we deal in apertures,
we say, in the business of proportional reveal.
Twice, that I know of, it falls into place: once,
when sand in mortar is listening to rain, and,
again, when slate roof tiles recall small words
in a ghost hand that rubbed them clean away.

Ben Wilkinson
The Nightmare

Remember that long drive back from the Lakes,
all lightning-lit through rolling rain?
Some nights I dream us on that stretch again,
the road like a river with a line of silver
fish that seem to leap about its centre;
leading us to Newby, Lawkland, Cleatop.

These times, though, the car shudders as if
someone about to collapse or vomit –
a thunderbolt, all cinematic flash,
throwing us forward through time
with the dashboard dials spinning;
making a DeLorean out of your Yaris.

The windscreen warps with scenery,
like some epic zoetrope at full tilt.
We watch the road narrow
into a dirt track, cars evaporate,
the trees shrivel into nothingness
while others burst up in their place.

Dumbstruck, we sit in its awful wake.
And I want to tell you that the world
we find is a glorious one,
some bucolic idyll bathed in light,
only I can't. Stepping out into heat
and a sky like hell, a murder of crows

screeches in the field to the west;
the trees all diagrams of hurt and harm,
the dry earth barren in an eerie calm.
Walking, a vast silence for what
seems like hours. Then, when I turn to
say as much, you're nowhere to be found.

By rights, that nightmare should end there.
Instead, on a kind of autopilot,
my dream-self carries on, hopelessly
trekking a dust trail. All to find nothing
aside that weird, familiar outline in the heat,
a shape on the horizon. It's then that I wake.

Sarah Corbett
An English Walk

The day's a beauty, sun on the minted
morning, a fresh hint of air from the west.
The climb up Steeple track, past the ox-eye
daisies, the piebald pony, the stone lintel
of the tumbled shack, takes nothing from you,
nor the sheep path that veers left over rough
ground to the lip, the brow, then the crown
of the hill. Now's the time to sit and draw
in the valley's veined cupola, the next
county's border a raised vernacular
after all those flat vowels. You'd been advised
to cross an unmarked field and cut the walk
a whole arduous mile; razor wire folds
loosely around bog grass and a haze lifts
from the soft ground. But how to do this –
slip past the way mark when you see the farmer
on the road and no convergent distance?
Now you are the girl who folds into a note
and posts herself skywards like a white bird.
You keep right and pass a farm where dogs
are set to guard at intervals in separate yards.
Allow now a long down hill, a rough jog
slowing as the road rises to the crossroads,
and although south rolls to a village,
you follow the map and set course north
for the plantation. It's midday, water's
low, your pack an extra kilo and lunch
must wait until you've placed a wall
between yourself and the curious cattle.
The walls are man-height, and you so small,
until the gate, tightly wrought barbed wire

and sheet iron layers over a nettled ditch.
She's back, the girl who can ride on air
and it's a snitch getting over this.
A cascade of tussocks on a sixty degree
slope and you've made it to the creek
where you unlace your boots and sink
your feet into the cool singing waters,
eat at last on the heat of the bank.
Lie down with the land now; you're halfway back.

Sharon Morris
Chorus

In this choiring, the soul looks upon the wellspring of Life — each scent of thorn separate, discriminate — froth of white flowers — hawthorn/quickthorn/whitethorn/blackthorn, May — Bend down — to the wash of blue, bluebell, Spanish/English (paler, more scented, prefiguring death) — to the lily, wood anemone, lesser/greater celandine, pink purslane, campion, violet/dog-violet, primrose/butter-rose (pink-eyed/thrum-eyed), cuckoopint/arum/lord and lady/Adam and Eve/bobbin/wake robin (spathe sheathed around spadix) — to the honey-sweet yellow anther, the pungent leaf of/stalk of ramson/wild garlic — the damp earth warm, well-lit before the canopy of leaf, sun after rain each twig and branch glassy — Look up through the cut buds/catkins, to new leaves — each blade velvet-bloom/shiny, serrated/smooth, holly/ilex — oval/boat/lobed — alder, beech/wild service, sycamore, maple, lime, London plane — pure//hybrid oak, common/uncommon, pedunculate/sessile, English/durmast, Turkey, American red, Cork//Lucombe — squint through the screen of set/array — compound leaflets alternate/paired opposing — mountain ash, false acacia/common ash — palmate chestnut horse/sweet, framing the light, dappling the sun — overlapping hands concealing blue, white/grey scudding clouds — Skying a mackerel sky, what individuates the haecceity of cloud? — pileus, pannus, velum, incus, mamma, virga, tuba, fumulus — be dazzled by the effects of light in air — halo, mock sun/sun-dog/parhelion, arc, corona, iris, glory — Listen to the volary, aggregation, roost, mess, leach, drove, aerie, rout, flew of birds — How many notes, mother? — lowing/bellowing of bullfinches, chime/family/herd of wrens, cloud/keg/merl of blackbirds, hermitage/mutation/rash of thrushes — calls of alarm/defence/attraction/mating/birth — contusion/mischief/tiding/charm/ tribe/murder of magpies — a *cri de coeur* — call and answer/hunger — chatter/clutter/hosting/murmuration/cloud/filth/scourge/congregation of starlings — too numerous to count, wing-beats imperceptible — charm/chirm/chirp of goldfinches, red-faced, wresting seeds from pine cones — jays/parakeets escaped from a circus — one pair of kestrels soaring, *kee kee, kee kee, kee kee, kee* — descant — veridical to that vernal sky — Hum of traffic in the distance — a woman strolls by learning a score by heart.

Plotinus *The Enneads* VI, 9, 9

Menna Elfyn
Arian Sychion

For Maha El Said

Hyd yn oed heb ei dolach yn ei ddwylo
  nid oes hafal i gyfalaf ambell ŵr.
Ac er mai i'r pant y rhed y dŵr,
  rhaeadr
sydd ar waelod tyle.

I hen wraig ar gyrion Cairo,
bydd yn golchi ei harian
yn foreol cyn eu rhoi
  ar lein ddillad-
  yn bapurau gwlybion.

Yno, byddant yn suo a siglo'n y gwynt
 cyn deffro ar eu hynt yn ddi-haint.
 Yn yr oes hon, rhaid sgwrio am arian
        glân

Filthy Lucre

A man has no need to rub his hands together
for others to know his wealth is unsurpassed,
and although money begets money
riches have wings.

On the outskirts of Cairo an old woman
washes her notes each morning,
then
hangs the wet papers out to dry.

There, they will whisper and sway on the wind;
next morning,
go out into the world, purified.

If you want your money clean these days, you must scour it yourself.

Translated by Elin ap Hywel

Casimiro de Brito
from The Art Of Dying Well

103

> *The bird of dawning singeth all night long.*
> *– Shakespeare,* Hamlet, *I,i*

Blind's the rutting that takes me inside
you, where you no longer are. I can hardly find
the void, the empty darkness. I hear birds
that no longer sing. And everything in me aches
when I go back to my sorrowful body
expiring beneath the last stars'
light. Less than a fallen
flower—less than a bee
that stung another life. I go back to death,
to the other name of mother in hopes
of finding something, some little bones
of eternity, a shell in which the world fits,
that's worth so little. Like someone taking
the instants he lived in the shadow of these trees
towards an island that no longer exists.
But the chaos, my love, the unloving,
how will I be able to praise it?

Translated by Louis Bourne

Emma Harding
What We Don't Admit To

after Cavafy

We've never done it
and (I'm almost certain)
we never will. But weeks
of lowered eyes, coded words,
charge the miles between us –
the phone in my pocket
a withheld sting.

Wine helps, of course
and so I stay too long
and imagine you understand
when I hug you a little too hard
needing to feel your body's flame
the graze of your stubble
your too-near lips.

Kathryn Simmonds
Experience

The widow will weep for her beau, my dear
While the spring grass continues to grow, my dear

Life's lengthy or short but it ends when it ends
We arrive and we go and that's so, my dear.

The elected must govern, the masses must vote
And a man has his price (*quid pro quo*, my dear)

But God seldom bargains and never in Lent
For he's too busy fighting the foe, my dear.

The moon eats her heart out again and again
But the rivers just go with the flow, my dear

An earthworm divides well, a country does not
And sometimes a yes becomes no, my dear.

Our wishes all fall down the well with a splash
There are decades of echoes but oh, my dear

Give up what is lost if you can't fish it back
Just keep walking. And that's all I know, my dear.

Diane Fahey
Respite Weekend

When I entered your room you'd cast off
the blankets, put the sheet over your face.
You were not dead, but wanted to be dead.
I lowered the sheet and kissed the white,
closed suffering of your face. It could make
no difference: you did not open your eyes...

I'd woken at six in a city hotel,
swum in the pool; then stood naked in my room,
writing the dream down lest it be
washed away by day's full light.

It can be almost time to die, one has
faced, accepted things – how one's life went,
present fear. But it's such hard work, Mother:
the waiting, the slow dying, the living on.

Martha Sprackland
The Swimming Pool

In the damp room beneath the pool
her swivel chair lolls, tracing
a slow arc one way, then the other
held on the pivot of a toe.
Already she's beginning to forget
the dripping attendant, and the officer
whose empty gun hung weighty
and defenceless.

On the other side of the door they talk in low voices
muffled by the chlorine.
He fills in a form, makes a call
the weight of the pool crushing him as it echoes
through the plumbing – the slap and
suck at the filters, the distorted voices
punctuated
by the clean knife of a body diving into water.

John Siddique
Perspective

In the heart of the leaf,
the tree.
In the heart of the tree,
the forest.
In the heart of the forest,
a silence/not silence.
In the heart of the silence,
a door.
In the room behind the door,
a woman and a man.
In the heart of the woman,
a girl.
In the heart of the man,
a boy.
'We must look after the children,'
they say over dinner.

Karen McCarthy Woolf
Portrait Of A Small Bird
On A Tree Of Twelve Metres

after Giuseppe Penone

I

Inside where it is dark, where branches
criss cross – a tree stripped

and whittled, where the wood is denser
and leaves flicker like bonfires

lit at the end of summer, here
in the heart of the wood you are the light

not the shadow, an unsolved equation
in a dog-eared exercise book.

II

Cross the red line and
the room changes size, dimension

– the ceiling reaches for a lightning spear,
wreaks havoc on a rectangle

of artificial daybreak while a rusted girder
snaps at a toddler on the bus –

everything I want is up there, just
out of reach, in the white emulsion.

CENTREFOLD

...Among ideas of England, time and space can manage a surprising (and sometimes impenetrable) elasticity: the past, as Michael Donaghy wrote, "falls open anywhere".

– *Sean O'Brien*

As Deep As England
From *The Newcastle / Bloodaxe Poetry Lectures 2011*

SEAN O'BRIEN

Ladies and Gentlemen, I hope you will forgive me if in this brief series of lectures I range quite widely, raising more questions than I seek to be able to answer, moving backwards and forwards in time, perhaps making connections without being able to pursue their implications properly. I've had to leave almost everything out. The subject, 'Ideas of England in Contemporary Poetry', is a large one, and it is also an area in which my own work as poet is engaged. So I'm partly on the inside of it myself. I am trying to find out what I think about it. If I knew the answer precisely, I might not be writing these lectures.

What does "England" mean? Well, as they say, if you have to ask... Yet it seems we do, perhaps especially in this period of rapid economic and social change, when the remains of the postwar settlement are impatiently dismantled and even to declare / accept / embrace a state of post-imperial modesty seems to be staking too large a claim on the world's attention and that of the markets who now govern us in all but name.

It could be objected that "England" and "Englishness" are not in themselves helpful ideas, that they resist clarification and contain too many internal contradictions, that the best way to understand a maze is perhaps not to go into it in the first place. But as I say, I am already inside the maze, imaginatively speaking, and have been at least since first I began to read and write poetry over forty years ago. My concern is with the workings of the imagination, which is not quite the same thing as the facts. The contradictions and paths into the mire and the grimpen, the dead ends and false trails, are part of the imagined England in which we live.

The poets with whom I began to read and study and write poetry – Ted Hughes and T.S. Eliot – are both heavily invested in ideas of England which, though in some ways very different from each other, also have common ground

This lecture was delivered by Sean O'Brien on 5 December 2011 as part of the *Newcastle / Bloodaxe Poetry Lectures Series*. It is published as *Journeys to the Interior: Ideas of England in Contemporary Poetry: Newcastle / Bloodaxe Poetry Lectures Series 12* (Newcastle / Bloodaxe, 2012).

in an enchanted or metaphysical notion of the place itself. So too does the poet who followed close on their heels in my reading, W.H. Auden, again ostensibly very different from the other two but drawn to the same ground, the common ground, perhaps, of their being. Many years later when I was writing a play about English Fascism in the 1920s and '30s, *Keepers of the Flame*, the hero found the image of what he wished to speak for at the heart of a wood in his native Northumberland: the resulting song was to bring him both fame and torment.

All interpretations, he may have felt, are misinterpretations. It may be too that in the individual and the collective imagination, some places seem more England than others. It might be reasonable to suspect that dwellers south of a line running from, say, Stratford-upon-Avon to London, feel themselves to be authentically English in a way that their neighbours to northwards seem to them not to be. And it's hardly necessary to remind an audience in Newcastle of the widespread instinctive sense in the North that *here* is clearly different from *down there* – yet at the same time it is England, perhaps for a northerner the *essential* presiding England, history notwithstanding. At one time not so long ago, some people liked to identify themselves as Northumbrians, but that making of an exception was also a claim to original authenticity, to having been in some sense here before the Normans, who are definitively "not from round here". The facts may argue differently, but England is a subject where the power of facts is quite limited. We are in the realm of belief and identity. The North, of course, still disproportionately supplies the armed forces with recruits – partly for economic reasons but partly too from identification with something almost beyond articulation that finds its most powerful emotional expression on occasions of national mourning and remembrance.

This lecture was written in part on Remembrance Sunday. There has been a good deal of public discussion this year about the wearing of poppies – by the England football team, by BBC presenters, by everyone else. There have been a lot of oughts about, a lot of they-should-be-made-to's. I have just read a news item from which I learn that some people are wearing larger poppies, or diamond encrusted poppies – presumably to indicate that they care more about the fallen than those who put their coppers in a street-seller's tin.

Where I live, spare diamonds are in relatively short supply, but on the way to the local churchyard for the ceremony of Remembrance I passed a teenage girl wearing a poppy pinned to her hat like a fashion accessory, and another with a poppy in her hair. I wasn't wearing a poppy myself, but my upbringing was traditional enough for me to have wondered momentarily if someone should suggest that they should put the poppy on the lapel, where it belongs. What someone? Where what belongs? Belongs to whom? In any case, what does the poppy now symbolise? Is it different from the blue cornflower worn by the French? I realised that, as so often happens by indirect routes, I was thinking about Englishness.

My attention was then distracted by further matters of protocol, manners, or as the current cant term has it, "appropriateness", by the sight of the elegant fortyish companion of a uniformed army colonel, making her way through the drizzle, furiously chewing gum. Good job she wasn't playing the bugle.

The event itself went off quite smoothly, though numbers were down because of the rain. The recent riots were also said to have failed to ignite in the North East because it was raining. As people walked home afterwards, they passed houses with flags of St George displayed in the upper windows. Ten years ago, hardly anyone would have known a flag of St George from a hole in the pavement, but ardent flag-wielders from the English Defence League were recently arrested in large numbers for trying to attack the anti-capitalist demonstrators encamped at St Paul's Cathedral. If it was necessary for the EDL to have a purpose other than a public ruck, it was presumably to defend England, but from what and in whose name? From the bankers? On the bankers' behalf?

England is in crisis, it seems. Who speaks for England? The famous phrase "Speak for England" (n.b. *not* "Speak for Britain") was uttered by the Conservative politician Leo Amery to indicate that by hesitating to declare war on Germany following the invasion of Poland in September 1939, the then Prime Minister Neville Chamberlain was failing to "speak for England". It was by all accounts a telling intervention, and it was Amery who some months later delivered the death blow to Chamberlain's premiership in the debate over military failure in Norway. He quoted Oliver Cromwell's words to the Long Parliament: "You have sat too long here for any good you have been doing. Depart, I say, and let us have done with you. In the name of God, go!" The last phrase is regularly parroted by less eloquent Members of Parliament to this day.

How complex "England" can prove to be is suggested by the fact that the intensely patriotic and imperialist Amery, opposed to appeasement of Hitler in the 1930s but favouring an alliance with Italy, was himself partly of Hungarian Jewish background and was the father of two notorious sons. One, John Amery, was hanged for treason at the end of the Second World War because of his active collaboration with the Nazis, including efforts to establish an English SS unit, the British Free Korps. The second was Julian

Amery, a right-wing Conservative minister with some reactionary political associates (and yet a member of the Special Operations Executive in wartime Yugoslavia). We seem to be a long way from poetry, but be assured we shall come to it: in England, of course, all roads lead to poetry.

Heinrich Heine wrote in *Religion and Philosophy in Germany*: "As soon as a religion seeks help from philosophy, its doom is inevitable. Trying to defend itself it talks itself further and further into perdition. Like any other absolutism, religion must not defend itself."[1] The same may hold true of ideas of nationality and national identity. I'm setting aside the issue of Britishness, which seems to divide rather than unite the population of the British Isles, in order to think about the equally intransigent topic of Englishness, with which Britishness is of course sometimes conflated. Heine also wrote that "Christianity is an idea, and as such indestructible and immortal, like every idea. But what is this idea?"[2] I would like to replace the word "Christianity" with the word "Englishness" here. And what *is* this idea, this Englishness? John of Gaunt's great deathbed speech in *Richard II* goes disregarded or uncomprehended by the self-absorbed king, who thinks, with one of his later European fellow-monarchs, "*l'etat, c'est moi*". Perhaps, though, he follows the grammatical shape of the old man's evocation:

> Methinks I am a prophet new inspired
> And thus expiring do foretell of him:
> His rash fierce blaze of riot cannot last,
> For violent fires soon burn out themselves;
> Small showers last long, but sudden storms are short;
> He tires betimes that spurs too fast betimes;
> With eager feeding food doth choke the feeder:
> Light vanity, insatiate cormorant,
> Consuming means, soon preys upon itself.
> This royal throne of kings, this scepter'd isle,
> This earth of majesty, this seat of Mars,
> This other Eden, demi-paradise,
> This fortress built by Nature for herself
> Against infection and the hand of war,
> This happy breed of men, this little world,
> This precious stone set in the silver sea,

1. Heinrich Heine, *The Harz Journey and Selected Prose*, Penguin, 1993 (2006) 'On the History of Religion and Philosophy in Germany', p.255.
2. ibid, p.206.

Which serves it in the office of a wall,
Or as a moat defensive to a house,
Against the envy of less happier lands,
This blessed plot, this earth, this realm, this England,
This nurse, this teeming womb of royal kings,
Fear'd by their breed and famous by their birth,
Renowned for their deeds as far from home,
For Christian service and true chivalry,
As is the sepulchre in stubborn Jewry,
Of the world's ransom, blessed Mary's Son,
This land of such dear souls, this dear dear land,
Dear for her reputation through the world,
Is now leased out, I die pronouncing it,
Like to a tenement or pelting farm:
England, bound in with the triumphant sea
Whose rocky shore beats back the envious siege
Of watery Neptune, is now bound in with shame,
With inky blots and rotten parchment bonds:
That England, that was wont to conquer others,
Hath made a shameful conquest of itself.
Ah, would the scandal vanish with my life,
How happy then were my ensuing death![3]

In the sentence stretching from "This royal throne of kings", the main verb is delayed for twenty lines. Clearly this intensifies the rhetorical impact, as image piles on image and we await the resolution, but it also leaves the evocation suspended without a governing tense, making "this England" a visionary state located neither in past, present nor future. Imaginatively this is a powerful position – that of the timeless, the immanent, the imminent, the possible – but in crudely political terms it is to the same extent vulnerable. It does not require proof, and it cannot supply any.

Qualities attributed to Englishness by politicians and others include democratic institutions, equality before the law, tolerance, sympathy for the underdog, fair play *et cetera* (Betjeman adds class distinction and proper drains). Depending on the national mood and the state of the economy and how much corruption is in the news this week, these claims may produce a certain amount of hollow laughter; and yet the qualities they refer to are

---

3. William Shakespeare, *Richard II*, Act II, Scene I, lines 31-68.

among those we would probably care to be identified with, aspirations to be borne in mind, however remote the possibility of their achievement may seem at any given point, as at the moment. But it is also probable that if the people of England – those who, according to G.K. Chesterton (who was fortunate to predecease local radio and the internet) have "never spoken yet",[4] were given the opportunity to decide, we should have capital punishment, closed borders, higher wages, lower taxes, an improved NHS funded by moonbeams, no arts funding and withdrawal from the EU. It begs the question of how *useful* an idea Englishness actually is. It might be truer to describe it as inescapable, like envy or the weather.

If there is always a mismatch between the desiderata and the day-to-day, there is also a tendency for notions of Englishness to sit more readily on the Right than the Left: it is a persistent tendency in Conservatism to view itself and Englishness as effectively synonymous, so that the one supplies the other's credentials and vice versa. It is to this end of the spectrum that a "platonic" England, a perfect original, permanently true and unchanging, also seems to belong. Its adherents can evince the Christianised class tribalism that once defined the Church of England as "the Tory Party at prayer". This end of the English spectrum may consider itself authentic and original, but it doesn't mind borrowing – 'Jerusalem', for example (William Blake may have been mad but he was no Tory), or the evocative passage from Orwell about spinsters cycling to Mass which was enlisted by the Conservative Prime Minister John Major as one of a number of recent doomed attempts to get hold of the idea of Englishness.

The symbolic capital of the Conservative tribe, its founding tradition, is rural and agricultural, however it has replenished or diminished itself by later involvement in industry and finance, and it is striking that the various myths I shall try briefly to evoke here all show an attachment to "the country" as a guarantor of authenticity and, in a sense, of originality. A titled lady, on hearing that Labour had won the 1945 general election, declared, "But the country won't stand for it". This is, you might say, the political form of the literary mode known as the Pastoral. The myths also involve an interesting circularity in that the rural world, governed by the seasons, is often also felt to be 'timeless'.

One thing that stands at the centre of the vexatious subject of England and Englishness is, of course, language. Its public uses are often, to put it mildly, impure. Repetition and distortion empty it of meaning. Few of those

---

4. G.K. Chesterton, 'The Secret People', line 2.

who use it for public purposes have any interest in or even any sense of language as something more than merely instrumental. "Language? Our Shakespeares will do that for us." Its aesthetic dimension is of little concern to them: at best it falls into the category of All Very Well – nice but inessential, like art, like culture – and if there is one word that has suffered terribly at the hands of ignorance and laziness lately, it is that word: culture. It will, we know, recover, with time, patience and perhaps a moratorium on its use. Ten years might do. I might place a modest bet with Paddy Power that after the 2012 Olympics we shall hear less of it.

I labour this introduction in order to suggest the kind of madly entangled briar patch into which the subject of Englishness seems to lead us, and to lead to the questions that animate these lectures. Within "culture", what do poets make of Englishness? What do they mean by it? Can they "speak for England"? Where is it? When is it or was it or will it be? Can it accommodate change and survive the apparent transfer of authority to Irish and Scots writers and other Anglophone writers further afield? Has it been left behind? Will it be abandoned? Must it be? Is it like the fossil in Peter Porter's poem that "ascends through slime / To selfhood and in dying finds a face"?[5] Or is there life in the old dog yet? With these things in mind, I want to sketch ideas of England as they manifest themselves in the poets who were most important to me in the years when I was beginning to write, and others who came close on their heels.

Ted Hughes's poem 'Pike' describes fishing at night for an ancient pike in a pond "as deep as England".[6] As a fourteen-year-old I found this a phrase of exciting resonance. Forty-odd years later I would say that the phrase works by identifying time with place, treating them interchangeably to reinforce each other's authority. And I would suggest that the whole mythological project of England works in the same way, whether in the clichés of the heritage industry or in the more exacting sphere of poetry. Shortly after I got to know Hughes's 'Pike' I read a comment by the poet-critic David Holbrook which dismissed that opening phrase – "It was as deep as England" – as an English equivalent of Welsh *hwyl*, by which he seems to have meant high-flown speech without substance, though that is not how it is defined in Welsh. This seemed rude not only to Hughes but also to the Welsh, and I have always instinctively resisted Holbrook's judgement.

As I began in my teens to develop an interior map of poetry (note the

---

5. Peter Porter, *The Rest on the Flight: Selected Poems*, Picador, 2010, 'Fossil Gathering', p.101.
6. Ted Hughes, *Collected Poems*, Faber, 2003, 'Pike', pp.84-85.

metaphor) this merger of place and time took on special prominence. To someone of my age, the indisputably great modern poet presented by the authorities (most notably Mr Grayson, my English teacher) was T.S. Eliot, an American who wanted to be English. After his re-conversion to Christianity, Eliot wrote insistently of the identical facts of place and time. Three of the *Four Quartets* take their titles from English placenames: 'Burnt Norton', 'East Coker' and 'Little Gidding'. (The fourth, 'The Dry Salvages', referring to a group of rocks off the Massachusetts coast, was once described by the English poet-critic Donald Davie as a parody.) East Coker, in Somerset, is currently under threat from a housing development. Some poets, though probably not Eliot, would think of this as the latest incarnation of the English curse of enclosure, although the place's defenders seem to see it in terms of "Heritage", which to some observers may seem like the "soft power" version of the same problem. All his English places were for Eliot sites of faith, of durable meaning, where, as he wrote, "History is now and England."[7] The transience of political concerns was trumped by the fact that what he found in his chosen places was, he felt sure, true.

His major successor, W.H. Auden, was also drawn to the imaginative authority with which an older world seemed charged. In his case it was a Norse saga-world that he situated in a country of his own devising, based in the lead-mining country of the North Pennines. Here the machinery of industry, whose very names seemed charged with religious significance, led backwards rather than forward. By the time Auden discovered the mines, they were already in decline, as though relics of the world of feuds and revenge about which he wrote in his early play, *Paid on Both Sides*. Limestone and the waters that ran through it and beneath it seemed a kind of guarantee on which an imaginative reality could be founded; and that folkloric world of saga and ballad gave access to certain mysteries which only the poet or the poem could properly enter. These form the ur-world of Auden's poems, and their very language is presented as existing at a level prior to or beyond rational interpretation.

In his book on the fundamentals of prosody, describing the intensified, ritualised attention produced by its organisation into lines, Alfred Corn writes: "poetry has never fully disengaged itself from its associations with shamanism; the poet, like the shaman, has mastered certain techniques – rhythmic, performative, imagistic, metaphoric – that summon the unconscious part of the mind, so that, in this dreamlike state between waking and sleeping, we

---

7. T.S. Eliot, *Collected Poems 1909-1962*, Faber, 1974, 'Little Gidding', p222.

may discover more about our thoughts and feelings than we would otherwise be able to do."[8] Even at his most seemingly rational-analytical, Auden is also serving a shamanic function, and the strongest truth-claims may in fact emerge from this necessarily occluded sphere. 'Oh where are you going?' is one of the most memorable and least self explanatory of the early poems:

> "Oh where are you going?" said reader to rider,
> "That valley is fatal where furnaces burn,
> Yonder's the midden whose odours will madden,
> The gap is the grave where the tall return."
>
> [...]
>
> "Out of this house" – said rider to reader;
> "Yours never will" – said farer to fearer;
> "They're looking for you" – said hearer to horror,
> As he left them there, as he left them there.[9]

John Fuller, in his invaluable *Commentary* on Auden, provides a convincing psychosexual decoding of this early (1931) poem but such analysis cannot help but seem reductive, because it must neglect the dramatising function of the poem's prosody – a ballad form subjected to heavy alliteration and other internal echoes, with simultaneous recurrence and variation of form and phrasing producing the effect of both repetition and instability, most notably in the final stanza, which both abandons the interrogative (change of form apparently indicating resolution) and refuses to answer the questions. The critic may read the poem as a disguise and seek to unmask its wearer, but poetically the disguise is the outcome, the *event*. The *event* of the poem, in which prosody is dominant, shows paraphraseable meaning overwhelmed by crisis (something which reaches an extreme development in the poems of James Fenton, who at one time seemed to be Auden's possible successor).

Auden's myth, like Eliot's, makes claims on history; and like Eliot's it also grants a kind of immunity from human time. A less intellectually ambitious poet, Philip Larkin, wrote of the same Pennine landscape as Auden in 'Show Saturday'. In Larkin's poem, actually based on Bellingham Show, in Northumberland, he notes that this public rural affirmation of skills and

---

8. Alfred Corn, *The Poem's Heartbeat: A Manual of Prosody*, Copper Canyon Press, 2008, p.6.
9. W.H. Auden, *Collected Poems*, Faber, 2007, 'Oh where are you going?', pp.59-60.

crafts and community is barely a day's length. Rather like the old high street butchers' and bakers' shops that always seemed no sooner to have opened than to be preparing to close, the showground crowd is soon on its way home. From halfway through the fourth of eight eight-line stanzas the end is taking place, as the horse-boxes, "like shifting scenery", slowly make their way:

> Back now to private addresses, gates and lamps
> In high stone one-street villages, empty at dusk,
> And side roads of small towns (sports final stuck
> In front doors, allotments reaching down to the railway);
> Back now to autumn, leaving the ended husk
> Of summer that brought them here for Show Saturday –
>
> [...]
>
> Back now, all of them, to their local lives [...]
>
> [...]
>
> To winter coming, as the dismantled Show
> Itself dies back into the area of work.
> Let it stay hidden there like strength, below
> Sale-bills and swindling; something people do,
> Not noticing how time's rolling smithy-smoke
> Shadows much greater gestures; something they share
> That breaks ancestrally each year into
> Regenerate union. Let it always be there.[10]

Englishness in poetry, it goes almost without saying, is often elegiac, its affirmations at their most powerful at the point of leave-taking. It may even have a death-wish secretly and pre-emptively inscribed within it. No sympathy with Larkin's politics is required to be moved by the extraordinarily vivid evocation mustered in 'Show Saturday', so much more powerful than anything Betjeman could create. "Let it always be there," Larkin ends. Yet compare the much inferior 'Going, Going', a rather muzzily unfocused protest against the perceived decline of the country into greed and vulgarity and ignorance, where Larkin fears that "that will be England gone".[11] Perhaps it would be true to say that for good and/or ill, it would be a *version* of England gone, a

---

10. Philip Larkin, *Collected Poems*, The Marvell Press and Faber, 1988, 'Show Saturday', pp.199-201.
11. ibid, p.189.

constellation of fetish-objects whose natural home is the correspondence columns of *The Daily Telegraph* and the irascible symposia of saloon bar philosopher-kings in the Home Counties. The vision sours when exploited.

Larkin was all too aware of time and mortality. In the absence of the religious convictions of Eliot and Auden, retrospect could never be enough, and anyway he lacked the materials and the required imaginative combination of luck, arrogance and endurance to create a mythology – and yet he is the most imitated poet of the three, and the best loved, which may make him more typical for the audience than the others.

These visions are all fundamentally rural (or even pre-urban). Eliot's visionary moments depend on such a context: for him the city is often a manifestation of Hell. Auden's Pennines are places from which the imagination derives and to which it returns for an image of underlying truth and authority ("What I see is a limestone landscape"[12]). Larkin laments a tradition broken, he imagines, by the First World War – "Never such innocence again"[13] – a conflict which marked the death of the notion of England as inherently or fundamentally rural. Yet the death of the idea did not kill off the attachment to it.

The First World War marked Ted Hughes's imagination very deeply. In one shocking phrase, he wrote that his father had been "heavily killed"[14] in the war (he had in fact survived but remained terribly damaged). Part of Hughes's response was to immerse himself ever more deeply in the rural, in isolated settings. One of these was the ancient Kingdom of Elmet, mysteriously situated anywhere from the borders of East Yorkshire to Halifax in the far west of the county. Its core, around Mytholmroyd and Hebden Bridge, is a zone where industry is seen, perhaps gratifyingly, declining into the earth from which it arose around the rivers of the Pennines. Political history has vanished entirely in Hughes's account. He also invested his imagination and his agricultural labour in the secretive valleys of Devon.

From these attachments in Hughes there emerges a fundamental dualism – on the one hand "the natural", on the other a preoccupation with violence which is both "natural" and at some level relishable. This blend is a kind of sophisticated atavism, the atavism of a poet who was as much a bookman as a naturalist. It's interesting in this respect to compare Hughes with a poet with a great deal more apparent warrant for an attachment to

---

12. W.H. Auden, *Collected Poems*, Faber, 2007, 'In Praise of Limestone', p.538-540.
13. Philip Larkin, *Collected Poems*, The Marvell Press and Faber, 1988, 'MCMXIV', p.127.
14. Ted Hughes, *Collected Poems*, Faber, 2003, 'Dust As We Are', p.753.

violence, his friend and collaborator Seamus Heaney, who laments the drowning of kittens and in sorrow and horror counts the cost of the violence done by people against other people. (The First World War is of course as powerfully remembered in the North of Ireland as in the North of England.) Born in 1930, Hughes missed both World Wars, as for various reasons did Larkin (unfit) and Auden (in the USA) and Eliot (too old) before him, but his imagination is a battlefield, where thistles are mown down as in "a feud" and are then seen "stiff with weapons, fighting back over the same ground."[15] Hughes also identified what he saw as the psychopathic Viking belligerence lightly submerged in the minds of Yorkshiremen, and as any Yorkshireman would tell you, Yorkshire is in fact really England, only better, and any doubts about this can be addressed in the carpark.

In his later years, as Poet Laureate, serving as poacher turned gamekeeper and as would-be national myth-maker (sometimes to the baffled scorn of the press), Hughes wrote of a distinction between historical time and the real, presiding extra-historical Time embodied in the person of the Queen Mother, which seems a grotesquely large amount of authority to invest in one very small person. This has the convenient effect – from a royalist point of view – of making politics irrelevant, though where it leaves the First World War is anybody's guess. But we don't, of course, look to poets primarily for logical constructions. They are imaginative rhetoricians, able, or at any rate often attempting, to bind or inhabit contradiction.

If it was possible to see Eliot, Auden and Hughes as, however variously, parts of the same enterprise, two of Hughes's contemporaries served to complicate matters. These were two Midlanders, raised in or near the fiery core of the Industrial Revolution. On the one hand we have Geoffrey Hill (b.1932), much of whose work seems oddly untouched by the city next door to his native Bromsgove, as was that of an earlier Bromsgrovian, A.E. Housman. On the other, we have Roy Fisher (b.1930) from Handsworth in the heart of Birmingham, who has written voluminously about the city he describes as "what I think with".[16]

In a dispute some years ago in the *London Review of Books*, Craig Raine took issue with Tom Paulin over Paulin's dismissal of Hill, claiming that there was something inherently English in Hill's work that Paulin, an Ulsterman and a republican socialist (actually born in York) was incapable of apprehending. At times, though, and not just to Paulin but to other unlucky

---

15. ibid, 'Thistles', p.147.
16. Roy Fisher, *The Long and the Short of It: Poems 1955-2005*, Bloodaxe, 2005, 'Texts for a Film 1: Talking to Camera', p285.

members of "lesser tribes without the law", the essentialist English Hill might seem rather like the Cheshire Cat, something that becomes invisible as it is looked at – though of course the Cheshire Cat is always smiling, which is not an accusation that can be levelled at Hill. Raine's recourse to essentialism might be seen as an act of critical desperation, an assertion of faith, a drawing of a line beyond which there can be no argument.

In what are perhaps Hill's most famous lines, from 'Funeral Music', his series of sonnets about the Wars of the Roses, the death of one England and the birth of another are focused at the ferocious battle of Towton, fought in a snowstorm on 29th March 1461, Palm Sunday, the warriors "livid and featureless, / With England crouched beastwise beneath it all. / 'Oh, that old northern business...'".[17] Twenty eight thousand men were at the time reputed to have died in this, the bloodiest battle of the extended civil war which was formally ended in 1485. Towton, interestingly, is near Sherburn-in-Elmet, which in name at least stands on the eastern edge of Hughes's imagined kingdom. It is also a place that visitors find still carries a chill, as of Wordsworth's "old, unhappy far-off things".[18] The site of battle itself is a low eminence of fields with no apparent horizons, with a concealed stream where the defeated Lancastrians were trapped and put to the sword by their Yorkist pursuers in a slaughter viewed as exceptional for the times, a fight to the finish where it was agreed in advance that there would be no quarter. The field of Towton is a landscape which seems both representative of "an idea of England", yet also, in its pitiless massiveness, more like "the vasty fields" of northern and central France to which many of the participants were ancestrally connected, than familiar images of rural England. As we seem somehow to be approaching deepest England, with its ancient strife and savagery, we find ourselves simultaneously in *la France profonde*. This is a connection scarcely to be admitted in public in England at present, when Francophobia seems, to those who voice it, more than ever self-evidently justified. But it's there, nevertheless. And rather than a single England, there may be Englands, like the 'Englands of the Mind' that Seamus Heaney wrote about in a famous essay on Hughes, Larkin and Hill, imagined places overlapping like a Venn diagram. And these Englands seek out their aptest forms in poetry.

While the work which made Hill famous is always conspicuously *made*, ceremoniously and brilliantly *achieved*, Roy Fisher writes an endlessly adaptable free verse, as if – paradoxically, given his work's Birmingham

---

17. Geoffrey Hill, *Collected Poems*, Penguin, 1985, 'Funeral Music', p.72.
18. William Wordsworth, 'The Solitary Reaper', line 19.

birthplace – it were the opposite of mass manufacture. Fisher's poems are often intensely seen yet rarely in a straightforward sense representational, and he delivers the following crisp and economical *non serviam* before the accumulated weight of English rhetoric:

> Because it could do it well
> the poem wants to glorify suffering.
> I mistrust it.
>
> I mistrust the poem in its hour of success,
> a thing capable of being
> tempted by ethics into the wonderful.[19]

There is no reason to suppose that Fisher has Hill in mind here, but it is interesting to consider that what Fisher seems to want to do is resist the reification of theme, place, feeling, attitude and conception of history that is always likely to accompany a poetic tradition. Another famous Fisher poem, 'For Realism', re-imagines an ordinary evening in the Midlands in visually empirical yet near-mystical terms, and presents a strange, tantalising parallel to the landscape and bloodstained snow of Hill's battlefield, in the vicinity of Lucas's lamp factory as the back shift comes off at 9pm:

> Above, dignity. A new precinct
> comes over the scraped hill,
> flats on the ridge get the last light.
>
> Down Wheeler Street, the lamps
> already gone, the windows have
> lake stretches of silver
> gashed out of tea green shadows,
> the after-images of brickwork.
>
> A conscience
> builds, late, on the ridge. A realism
> tries to record, before they're gone,
> what silver filth these drains have run.[20]

---

19. Roy Fisher, *The Long and the Short of It: Poems 1955-2005*, Bloodaxe, 2005, 'It is Writing', p.221.
20. ibid 'For Realism', pp.220-221.

Compare this to the third section of 'Funeral Music':

> They bespoke doomsday and they meant it by
> God, their curved metal rimming the low ridge [...]
> With England crouched beastwise beneath it all [...]
> Among carnage the most delicate souls
> Tup in their marriage-blood.[21]

On the far side of the sense of suffocation and confinement and loss of energy that helped lead Pound and Eliot into modernism stands Fisher's work. Where the founders of poetic modernism either broke or rewrote tradition the better to come at a history which habit and rhetoric had obscured, Fisher arrives as a poet in the middle of the twentieth century, and the history that most interests him is the history of the present, his own immediate world and lifetime, with the Second World War as perhaps a starting point and very little before it seeming to find its way into the poems. (Since Fisher's retirement, of course, he has written evoking more remote periods, in landscapes – the western Peak District – which seemingly encourage him to do so.) A man born amid industry may feel little connection to the world of before – his own class may have been swiftly disconnected from it – before Birmingham became the fiery metropolis of unceasing hammer-blows. Shakespeare's home landscape may be only a bus-ride away, but as we have seen, among ideas of England, time and space can manage a surprising (and sometimes impenetrable) elasticity: the past, as Michael Donaghy wrote, "falls open anywhere".[22] To close with, a Fisher poem from the mid-sixties seems to draw tantalisingly together various of the themes and attitudes I've referred to. This is 'An English Sensibility', and it ends:

> Out in the cokehouse
> cobweb
> a dark mat
> draped on the rubble in a corner
> muffled
> with a fog of glittering dust
> that shakes
> captive

---

21 Geoffrey Hill, *Collected Poems*, Penguin, 1985, 'Funeral Music', p.72.
22. Michael Donaghy, *Collected Poems*, Picador, 2009, 'Black Ice and Rain', p.124.

in the sunlight
over pitted silver-grey
ghost shapes that shine through.[23]

"Ghost shapes", "a fog of glittering dust", – sometimes that seems to be what we're trying to get hold of.

Sean O'Brien is Professor of Creative Writing at Newcastle University. His sixth collection, *The Drowned Book*, won the 2007 Forward and T.S. Eliot Prizes. His latest collection, *November*, was published in 2011.

---

23. Roy Fisher, *The Long and the Short of It: Poems 1955-2005*, Bloodaxe, 2005, 'From an English Sensibility', p.251.

Poetry Despite The Fact(s): Contemporary Greek Poets

SELECTED AND INTRODUCED BY SOCRATES KABOUROPOULOS

"There were signs that Greece was going to default, but no-one paid any attention," said the front page of the *International Herald Tribune* during November 2011. For the past two years, the connotations of the word "default" have been haunting everyone who lives in the country. Indeed, how can an entire country "default"? And are all its individual citizens to blame (unavoidably reading "responsibility" as guilt)? While all Greeks have felt, more or less, the pressure to respond to this spur, it is interesting to see how the current crisis is perceived and adopted by authors. Does it affect literary creation, and if so in what ways?

In his famous lecture presenting 'Six Greek Poets' in January 1971, when the military dictatorship was almost dying out, the American critic Kimon Friar referred to the imagery, technology and pop culture influences, and the deliberate shaping of poems like jigsaw puzzles, which characterised the emergent "70s Generation": a new wave that would thoroughly renew Greek poetry. Their direct relationship to mythology, feminism and political awareness, as well as to Solomos, Cavafy, Kazantzakis and the Greek surrealists of the 1930s, was also noted by other critics. While four of those six poets are no longer alive,[1] the remaining pair – Katerina Anghelaki-Rooke and Lefteris Poulios – and their contemporaries count among the most important Greek poets today.

Katerina Anghelaki-Rooke's (b.1935) latest book of poetry is titled *The Anorexia of Existence* (2011). In it, the promethean power of the joy of life and love, so vividly present in all her work, is substituted with the "snakes" of the subconscious, which are supposed to warn us against the coming of old age and our lack of resilience. However, the vanity of erotic delusion has been a constant theme in all Anghelaki-Rooke's work. In her poetry she has developed both a euphoric erotic realm, and a reflective detachment from it, through concepts derived from mythology and from a female existential view.

Christophoros Liondakis's (b.1945) latest, prize-winning collection, published in 2009, bears the significant title *At Delusion's End*. A prominent

---

1. Tassos Denegris, Vassilis Steriadis, Nana Issaia and Dimitris Potamitis.

poet of the seventies, Liondakis calls for a moral stance to be adopted in difficult circumstances, and developed at a non-superficial level: a personal purging, in the form of "ridding oneself of thorns". Many currents meet in the poem selected for publication here – from Fyodor Dostoyevsky's Rodion Romanovich Raskolnikov to the origins of Christianity – while their combination with repressed male sensuality relates directly to the work of C.P. Cavafy.

By contrast George Veis (b.1955), also a writer of the seventies, has continuously transformed his poetry in order to adopt a more meditative approach to images of cities and nature, experienced as states of mind. Having lived for many years in the Far East, serving as a diplomat (he is the Greek ambassador in Indonesia, today), in *N, As In Nostalgia* (2009), Veis seems to adapt and, at the same time, to detach himself from the Eastern poetry tradition, reverting to the poetics of space and time of the pre-Socratic philosophers like Heraclites and, especially, Parmenides.

The appearance, at the beginning of the eighties, of Haris Vlavianos (b.1957), who read Philosophy at Bristol University, and History and Political Science at Oxford, marks a decisive turn towards a less openly (or rhetorically) emotional and more philosophic poetry, in constant discussion with the Western tradition. In his latest volume, *Sonnets of Despair* (2011), the poet's personal intimate confessions are challenged by a profound questioning of reality and its openness to misinterpretation(s), giving them a high level of sophistication and fragility.

In the work of a younger generation of Greek poets who first emerged in the nineties, reflective as well as performative patterns become more common. For Phoebe Giannisi (b. 1964), a professor of Architecture at the University of Thessaly, a background counting of the words, and their symmetry, pace and prosody, becomes an ironic vehicle with which to relate herself to a living "ancient" past. Even more elaborate, the poetry of Katerina Iliopoulou (b. 1967) calls for a desperate need to "decipher" landscape, questioning the nature of its perception. "Nature is the field where the senses are being tested and landscape a book that needs to be read," she indicates, creating a breathtaking narrative in her *Book of Soil* (2011).

Turning to the poets who were born after 1970, and who are, more or less, now publishing their first books, the stage becomes even more intercultural, diverse and vibrant. This selection includes the perfectly bi-lingual Krystalli Glyniadakis (b. 1979), an LSE graduate in Political Philosophy who writes in Greek and in English and has attended creative writing courses in the UK, whose poetry is intelligent, humorous, rigorous and at times sensual; the prize-winning young poet and London resident Thodoris

Rakopoulos (b. 1981), who combines imaginative syntheses with a revisiting of political awareness; and Stamatis Polenakis (b. 1970), whose sensibility in respect to objects and figures of the past activates a lyric impulse, questioning the present through a depiction of decay and loss, in a narrative both formal and profound.

Socrates Kabouropoulos (b. 1962) is a poet, translator and works at the National Book Centre of Greece. Between 2009-2011, he co-organised the Greek-American Poetry Meetings in Paros and in Delphi.

Christoforos Liondakis
Ridding Oneself Of Thorns

Bronze in the Museo dei Conservatori but elsewhere too.
Spinario is the name always given to you.
With your left foot on your right knee
you are ridding yourself of thorns.
In the same position you're depicted in a corner of the icon.
It's in this position I see Rodion Romanovich
ridding himself of feelings of guilt.
The waiter at four in the morning
ridding himself of sweat-drenched socks.
The bather on the beach at Althaia
ridding himself of clinging pitch.
Aglaios before the frozen lake
ridding himself of his uniform.
Mike Tyson ridding himself of his boxing gloves.
In this same position, in the park at dusk,
I see you ridding yourself of envy.

From *At Delusion's End*, 2010, translated by David Connolly

Haris Vlavianos
Sonnets Of Despair, III

I am holding in my hands the pictures
from our last summer in Pesaro.
You couldn't imagine then – neither could I –
that nine months later you would be dead.
I am looking at your face leaning tenderly against mine.
It is the face of a stranger, not the one reflected in my gaze,
that sunny day, outside Rossini's house.
As if death came in the meantime and coloured your eyes
 – these eyes that had enchanted so many in the past – with another shade,
as if your smile were no longer a smile,
but the grimace of a spectre. The make-up artist did a good job.
With his experienced, ghastly touch
he managed to transform your image.

It is as if you were never alive. You never were.

From *Sonnets of Despair*, 2011, translated by the author and Mina Karavanta

Katerina Iliopoulou
How To Walk In A Field

Although there is no door / we entered somewhere.
Immediately we came across the process of transformation.
A crowd of tiny birds (invisible before) left the ground
Touching the tips of wheat.
This way making them breathe
Making them participants in flight.
Every stalk of wheat seemed to give birth to a bird.
Finally they stopped.
No one was left.
We still did not know how to proceed
With our question ripe in our hands.
If it were a well we could throw a stone
And wait for the answer
Or maybe it would be enough to retract some evidence
(Plants, some soil)
To extract our conclusions.
That is to say with attacking or stealing.
We decided to forget ourselves inside our small choreography.
Forgetting as well as entering is a kind of departure.
What were we to leave behind?
Gigantic thistles of satiate orange colour
Were turning their heads to the faint wind
As if they were about to move forward.
In the whole place as we were approaching
What we would call centre,
There was but the sense of beginning.
The field was a closed fist that would not show.

From *The Book of Soil*, 2011, translated by the author and Edward Smallfield

Phoebe Giannisi
Thinking

death doesn't exist Epicurus said because when we are alive we are in
life and don't know death whereas afterwards we die we are no more
and so death to us cannot be he said all this because he knew that we
are aware that we will die this makes us differ from the rest of the
animals his words and his thinking apply to the animals too if of
course they were thinking though if they could think they too would
be in our position because they would know the future thinking
means to project projecting means changing position within time or
in space according to Nietzsche the happiness of animals is founded
on their lack of memory so the present is strictly the present but
man constantly sees the present through the past but also sees the
present through the future the question is does he ever see the
present through the present what does the moment mean to him as
he experiences it might it be what he has already forgotten we live as
immortals knowing well we are mortal man is a strange animal

Translated by Katerina Iliopoulou, Socrates Kabouropoulos and Andrew Maxwell

Stamatis Polenakis
Photograph Of Vacationers In The Russian Countryside

Where, I wonder, are those melancholy girls of ephemeral youth?
Olga, Irina and Masha, feeble autumn trees,
remember the names of all those who once rested in your shade,
have no more regrets for the years that slip by,
I myself have no other way,
I too embraced these trees with trembling hands,
I too loved unattainable eternity.
There is no other time for me except this past that continuously drifts away,
there is no other way for us Olga, Irina, Masha,
I have never understood death.
And I too furiously strike the earth with my cane, helpless, like a blind man.

From *Notre Dame*, 2008, translated by Richard Pierce

Krystalli Glyniadakis
If We Are Shades
(Variation On A Theme By Carol Ann Duffy)

If we are shades
Who walked here once
Among the concrete buildings, on guiding streets
Hot in our skin and hearts
With all the time we thought was left to us

If we were there
Just in time, breathing still
Our countable days
The words exchanged
The laughter released
Parting defences with our teeth

Would you rather be here
Than where you are and where I'm
Still ahead
If we are bodies
Who lived love
Before we are long dead

Thodoris Rakopoulos
Without Words

(caption in a poem)

The look is visible here,
almost touchable,
recognisable; entirely hers.

You make her out in the joints,
in the stitching you feel the swishing,
the thread the fabric the garment bear

the invisibility of her writing's ink.
She passed along leaving
words behind as excreta.

From these by going backwards
we found ourselves at this opening: here
the landscape balanced in mid-air

any human addition
could have spoiled it
that's why we traversed it with bated breath

until we went astray
in this
poem.

Signatures follow.

From *Fayyoum*, 2010, translated by Yannis Goumas

George Veis
Time's (Simple) Annulment

"Amid the orange tree's leaves
day passes, cleaning its wings
silver words sway: midday.
With right hand you indicate the sea,
an absence of matter, tomorrow you'll call it
departure. The wind blows,
my ears filled with dust, truth's filter."

I wrote and remained there.
Let me recall still recall:

"My ears filled with truth, sand's filter
the wind blows, return
a presence, matter, tomorrow you'll call it
sea (again and again)
with left hand I indicate
my silver seconds –
how they roll, how they return here where I am,
breakfast in Cairo or Folegandros in mind –
always the same hawk passes
cleaning its wings in the rain's wake
timeless."

I write and remain here
a present
never-ending.

From *N, As In Nostalgia*, 2009, translated by David Connolly

Krystalli Glyniadakis
Mr Nietzsche

A lack of a system is all very well,
Mr Nietzsche
    (and so damned honest – no doubt about it –
    since the mind is such a muddle
    and the uttered thoughts are weapons –
    sharp, inadequate)

but was all that perhaps merely an excuse
so that others could do the dirty work?

For nothing is more exasperating
than a slothful hand
and a bunch of people demanding
    an explanation
    an explanation!
so you end up saying what you didn't want to say at all
so you end up forgetting
and end up getting muddled.
And what's more, they blame you
for your lack of rhythm and clarity, *for your lack of weapons.*
As if the world were a well-tuned clock.

So – you said – it's better to write just as it comes
and let others pull the chestnuts out of the fire.

I know what I want to say,
I know what I believe in. How well I know
what pitfalls are in store for lovers
of truth and clarity.
Whoever wants to find out
has to go it alone.
I can't be bothered with plumbing the depths of my mind.
(To say nothing of this world.)

Weapons only lead to pointless and brutal wars.

From *London–Istanbul*, 2009, translated by Richard Pierce and Stamatis Polenakis

Katerina Anghelaki-Rooke
Our Friends The Snakes

Perhaps the snakes that encircle us
are creatures benevolent
and useful
since they liberate our suspicions
from promises that are fake.
And as they writhe
they teach us that no reality
is more precious, and more real
than the breath of the moment.
What did the people promise you?
A sweet life?
But this needs huge imagination.
What did the saints promise you?
An eternal life?
But this needs a huge resilience.

From *The Anorexia of Existence*, 2011, translated by the author and Costas Nisiotis

Socrates Kabouropoulos
EU=KALON (In Greek: Beautiful)

he stares at me with his dark blue eyes, a pair of
silent half-moons

*

he stares into my eyes, his eyes both calm and inquisitive
lying on my chest, he falls asleep

*

only in his dreams does he smile

*

a child, Lem's idea of the 'ocean' in miniature (as in *Solaris*); it
mirrors our inner thoughts, worries, aspirations, guilt; in itself,
the incarnation of a dream

*

"size makes no difference for beings of the same kind,"
says the doctor

*

they showed the same knowing dismay towards life, in the line
of their lips

*

he raises his head towards the light, at pains,
like a worm, a snail, a turtle

*

I look at him, forehead weary; the sparkle in his eyes brings me back

Texts With And Without Context: Youth Poetry In Beirut

OMAR SABBAGH

At first, life was simple; life was an umbrella that protected our serendipitous
fruit
And with and within our life we used to draw white dreams along the rims of
volcanoes
And between the flames and our cold beds we were inhabited by joy.
– Ali Zaraket, 'Life was Simple...'

Last September I moved to Beirut, the Lebanon, to take up a visiting teaching position at the American University of Beirut. By October, I had already lived my way into a groove of work alternating with soused relaxation. One evening I entered a restaurant round the corner from my apartment and saluted the owner, who I knew and to whom I'd given a copy of my first collection. Taking my seat at the bar I was immediately introduced to the young man sitting next to me, as one "poet" to another.

Ali Zaraket is a twenty-nine-year-old poet based in Beirut. A couple of weeks after our meeting, I sat with him in a pub in the hub (*Hamra*) of Beirut. Over the course of an hour I was able to gain an insight into the youth poetry scene here, of which he is eminently representative.

Zaraket has already made his mark as a poet. He has been published in the major newspapers (there are no specialist poetry journals here), such as *Al-Hayat*, *Al-Mustakbal*, *Al-Safir* and *Al-Nahar*, and is the author of two books, *Kitab Farigh* (*Empty Book*) and *Kannit al-Hayat Rakhwa* (*Life Was Simple...*).

The title of Zaraket's first book suggests the idea of the *tabula rasa* or "blank cheque" of youth (the book being the self), which is to be filled and / or fulfilled in time. Indeed, some of the text of this first book builds on sentences written at the age of nine, when Zaraket began to write: the rawness of that as yet unfulfilled state being unrecoverable. Interestingly, this first volume is printed in the author's own cursive, and illustrated with his line drawings. There is the sense, as he showed me, of both continuity and discontinuity. As T. S. Eliot noted in 'Tradition and The Individual Talent', such discontinuity or change in images across the arc of a book is only possible due to an overall identity, executive authority or overarching "intentionality".

This "life" – for surely this text across/through context is precisely how (human/symbolic) life is lived – is also apparent in his relationship to the Arabic language. Not only does Zaraket write in the Lebanese idiom, rather than the classical/literary language, but he also talks of his praxis as a poet as breathing contemporary life into the (sacred or not) Arabic. Arabic, as I have always suspected, and as he agreed with some excitement, is a far less alienated language than say, contemporary French or English. Words in Arabic are poetically rich and overcharged with equivocation and plurality of meaning, due to remaining within the concrete and storied context (*mythoi*) in which they originated. Interestingly, Zaraket described his use of Arabic in delimiting his contemporary life as "archaeological" work. In other words, as in the logical shape of Eliot's insight, one can only create something "new" or unique to a voice out of something "shared" and objective.

And yet, for all the fecund polymorphousness of the language, Zaraket told me that when the young want to discuss relationships, especially sexual or romantic relationships, they speak in English, finding, as Wittgenstein attests, the context and life-world of that language-game (say) more apt for the subject. Although an atheist and a libertarian, he accepts that moderate and organic Islam would or should be the natural source of mores, not necessarily political institutions, in the Middle East. And this, *especially* given the contemporary fear in the West that the Arab Spring will result in Islamic parties gaining new ground in the various states involved.

When I asked what poetry is to him, Zaraket, reminding me of the eleventh chapter in Augustine's *Confessions*, suggested it was a tool to capture the present of existence. Which is to say, that clothing time in verse gives one purchase, "ex-static" or not, on the evanescence of time as experienced. And yet, unlike Augustine, stilling time thus takes the place of any transcendent absolute which, otherwise, would be the source and guarantor of meaningful expression.

Text or quiddity is seen to be a derivation of or variation on a shared life-world. However, this Lebanese context is specified as the sharing of something essentially fractious: a continuity made up of ruptures. When I asked about the youth (say, twenty- to forty-year-old) poetry scene in Beirut, Zaraket was more despondent. Although his personal creative process, that of distilling a contemporary idiom from a sacred/ancient language, involves creating texts out of an objective context, he told me that as a "scene" or "literary community", Beirut was eminently anomic. According to Zaraket, there is far more of a publishing "scene" (with publishers such as Dar al-Jadeed, Al-Farabi, Dar Al-Nahda Al-Arabeeya, Aj-Jamal and Riyad Rayiss) than any poetry "scene". This is not surprising to anyone who knows the entrepreneurial panache of the Lebanese.

Indeed, Zaraket's portrayal of the praxis of Lebanese poets was both agonistic, and antagonistic. The Lebanese context is one of "unending tragedy", and this sense and historic context informs both the lives of the poets and the life of the poetry; due to the anomie of such a rife history and present, each poet is a text without a unified or meta-narrative. For Zaraket, poets here are individual writers, and readers are inevitably individual readers.

Furthermore, poetry is complicated in the Arab world by the split between the social "tone" of the various states. In the more conservative states of the Gulf, for instance, poets use traditional metres and forms; similarly there are still those within such a disenchanted and worldly city as Beirut who work almost exclusively within traditional forms. However, Zaraket and his peers inherit the non-restrictive *vers libres* which became widespread during the seventies in the Arab poetry world. Significantly, Zaraket says that this split is almost absolute; there is no sense of a common heritage or present situation. As ever, like Lebanese to Lebanese, Arab to Arab is not the most easeful story.

The poets suggested as Zaraket's peers include names such as Mazen Ma'rouf, Samer Abou-Hawash, Rami Al-Amin, Fidel Sbeiti, Joumana Haddad, Nazem Al-Sayyed, Samar Abdel-Jaber and Yehia Jabber. The latter is "one of the most vivid, modern and moving of poets in contemporary Arabic", according to Zaraket. Although these poets all know each other, their poetic praxes can be seen as a series of truncated attempts at representing or expressing what is to a certain extent abject and unspeakable.

In fact, it is precisely this "existential" factor, this "sublime" factor to life in Lebanon, which I find missing in my own work as a poet. Like Israelis, Lebanese live for the moment, jaundiced by decades of foreign interference and sectarian troubles. Indeed, I remember friends telling me that in the recent (summer 2006) war with Israel, the young continued to party at night while Beirut was being bombed. A sense of risk or urgency (and concomitant *sang froid*) informs life here. On the other hand, I was born and grew up in England in an upper middle class family in the wake of the Lebanese Civil War – in a bubble so to speak; a bubble which to this day allows me to be precious and extremely self-indulgent on occasion, whereas the exigencies of Lebanese life seem, in my eyes, to offer a justification of all Lebanese woebegone expressions. My conversation with Zaraket was, thus, a lesson in humility.

Zaraket was born just after Israel invaded Lebanon in the early eighties. He experienced civil war at first hand in his earliest years. And then there was the war with Israel in 1993, when Israel occupied the Lebanese south. Further catastrophes occurred throughout the nineties and into the early twenty-first century. Most recently, there was the thirty-four day war in July 2006, about which the epigraph to this article speaks in a protean, readied and very Lebanese spirit.

Adorno said famously that after the *Shoah*, lyric poetry – the dramatisation of spontaneous individuality and individual feeling – was impossible. Death, previously the guarantor of meaningful individual life, had become absolutely arbitrary. And yet, in dialectical fashion – one extreme implying its opposite extreme – he later changed his mind. Although not on the scale of the Holocaust or the Palestinian tragedy (*al-Nuqba*), the Lebanese live, to a certain extent, a hunted life. My time spent with Zaraket was both a meeting of minds and also a setting for stark contrast, a chiaroscuro of discretely exclusive life-worlds.

Omar Sabbagh's *My Only Ever Oedipal Complaint* was published in 2010 (Cinnamon). His second collection, *The Square Root Of Beirut*, is published by Cinnamon.

Yehuda Amichai
The Jewish Time Bomb

On my desk is a piece of stone engraved *amen*,
one survivor of the thousands and thousands of fragments from graves
in Jewish cemeteries. And I know that all the shards
are filling up the biggest Jewish time bomb
together with other splinters, fragments from the Tables of the Law,
filling it with broken altars and crosses, rusty crucifix nails,
and broken bones, broken holy vessels, broken houseware,
and shoes, glasses, artificial limbs, dentures,
and empty canisters of lethal poison: all these
are filling up the Jewish time bomb until the end of days.
And even though I know about these things and about the end of days,
this stone on my desk gives me tranquility.
It is a stone of truth left to its own devices,
wiser than any philosopher's stone, a stone from a fractured grave
and this stone is absolutely perfect,
this stone testifies to all the things that have ever existed
and all the things that will exist for ever, an Amen stone and love.
Amen, amen and may this be His will.

Translated from the Hebrew by Anthony Rudolf and Miriam Neiger-Fleischmann

Note: 'The Jewish Time Bomb' is the final poem in Yehuda Amichai's final book. This new translation was specially prepared for an installation by the Israeli poet and painter Miriam Neiger-Fleischmann, and included in her exhibition at the Jewish Museum in Budapest (March 2010).

THE NATIONAL POETRY COMPETITION 2011

Allison McVety, Samantha Wynne-Rydderch and Zaffar Kunial are the winners of the National Poetry Competition 2011. Here, each of this year's judges, Jackie Kay, John Glenday and Colette Bryce, talks about one of the winning poems.

Jackie Kay on Allison McVety's winning poem, 'To the Lighthouse'
"We admired the way this poem achieves several things at once. It makes you remember that strange sensation of returning to a book to find it altered, only to realise the book hasn't changed: you have. It makes you re-appreciate Virginia Woolf and deals very subtly with her suicide. "Everything big happens in parenthesis", is as much about Woolf's death as it is about the poet's mother's. And the image of the brackets in the water at the end is terribly moving. In three stanzas, this poem captures not just the movement of time (that so obsessed Woolf) but also the passing of time in the poet's life, the journey from the girl in her exams, to the motherless woman at the end. It's a poem that takes huge leaps and yet shimmers with small details. It is a meta-poem."

John Glenday on Samantha Wynne-Rydderch's 'Ponting'
"There's a trick a great poem pulls. Somehow or other it stops being just stains on paper and opens a window through which we can stare, drawn in by the newly familiar. Great poems accommodate scrutiny – the viewpoint shifting slightly, perspectives deepening the more we gaze. I came across this poem buried deep in the welcome blizzard of submissions. A blink of Antarctic light, it shone out, and kept on shining. 'Ponting' is witty, enchanting, beautifully constructed, meticulously observed. A poem of wisdom, dedication, and most of all, a genuine love for its subject."

Colette Bryce on Zaffar Kunial's 'Hill Speak'
"We were intrigued by the linguistic trail laid down in the speaker's search for his roots in language. Each time we read it, we noticed new connections, and the space created by the poem seemed to open up. We wanted to read it again, and again. In the strange business of competition adjudication, that counts for such a lot."

FIRST PRIZE

Allison McVety
To The Lighthouse

i The Window

It was Virginia's charcoaled stare
that put me off: her disappointment
in me, the reader, before I even started.
So I walked into the exam without her:
without the easel, the skull or the shawl,
the well-turned stocking, Minta's
missing brooch. In the hall I watched
the future show its pulse and all the girls,
the girls who'd read the book, set off
together, lined up at desks and rowing.

ii Time Passes

You need a *daubière* and too much time –
three days' absence from the plot. Rump
bathed overnight in brandy, a stout red
brought back from France. The liquor's
boiled once, added back to beef, calf's foot,
lardons, *les legumes*. For six hours – or more –
it idles. It can't be over-cooked. It will not
spoil. At table, a stream of consciousness
breaks out. And it rains. It rains. If not
the stew, what was the woman on about.

iii The Lighthouse

The year I gave the book another go,
[the year my mother died], I learned
everything big happens in parenthesis –
marriage, birth, The War, poetry. Is it the full
manuscript or just the bits in the middle
that count. Is it the woman at the window,
marking the hours, from cover to cover –
or these few lines: that as she eased out from
the bank and into the water the brackets
of it opened and closed about her.

NATIONAL
POETRY
COMPETITION

THE
POETRY
SOCIETY

The Poetry Society, and judges Colette Bryce, John Glenday and Jackie Kay, congratulate the following poets on their success in the National Poetry Competition 2011:

FIRST PRIZE
Allison McVety – 'To the Lighthouse'

SECOND PRIZE
Samantha Wynne-Rhydderch – 'Ponting'

THIRD PRIZE
Zaffar Kunial – 'Hill Speak'

COMMENDED
Lindy Barbour – 'White Basin'
Liz Berry – 'Birmingham Roller'
Antony Dunn – 'In Vitro'
Rosalind Hudis – 'Photograph'
Helen Klein Ross – 'How to Furnish an American House'
S.J. Litherland – 'Springtime of the Nations'
Ian McEwen – 'Our Lady of the Pylons'
Jon Stone – 'Blue Poison Dart Frog'

For information on the National Poetry Competition, visit the Poetry Society's website **www.poetrysociety.org.uk**

SECOND PRIZE

Samantha Wynne-Rhydderch
Ponting

In the end we turned him into a verb:
to pont meaning *to pose in ice and snow*

until frozen. On the voyage south he'd be
tilting plates in the darkroom, in one hand

the developing dish, in the other a basin
of vomit. One minute he'd arrange us

in groups for the cinematograph, then rush
to the ship's side. Once Ponco roped up

his JA Prestwich over *Terra Nova*'s bow,
balanced on three planks. He lost the tip

of his tongue when it stuck to the camera
at thirty below. Corneas can freeze

to peep-sight. At one hundred degrees
of frost the film's ribbon will split.

To pont would also mean *pontificate.* He'd insist
on reeling the film slowly to prevent

sparks. We'd rehearse the Pole Picture:
mount the camera on the theodolite tripod,

wind twine over the trigger and guide it
round a ski stick to get the direction right.

He'd instruct us on setting the shutter, how to
use a flash in the tent with quarter of an inch of powder

and F11. En route to the Pole I sent back
negatives with the support teams, a sheet

torn from my sledging log detailing exposure
data; how composed we were, how cold.

THIRD PRIZE

Zaffar Kunial
Hill Speak

There is no dictionary for my father's language.
His dialect, for a start, is difficult to name.
Even this taxi driver, who talks it, lacks the knowledge.
Some say it's Pahari – 'hill speak' –
others, Potwari, or Pahari-Potwari –
too earthy and scriptless to find a home in books.
This mountain speech is a low language. *Ours.* "No good.
You should learn speak Urdu." I'm getting the runaround.

Whatever it is, this talk, going back, did once have a script:
Landa, in the reign of the Buddhists.
... So was Dad's speech some kind of Dogri?
Is it Kashmiri? Mirpuri? The differences are lost on me.
I'm told it's part way towards Punjabi,
but what that tongue would call *tuvarda*,
Dad would agree was *tusaana* –
'yours' –

truly, though there are many dictionaries for the tongue I speak,
it's the close-by things I'm lost to say;
things as pulsed and present as the back of this hand,
never mind stumbling towards some higher plane.
And, either way, even at the rare moment I get towards –
or, thank God, even getting to –
my point, I can't put into words
where I've arrived.

REVIEWS

... rings and standing stones, the turfed mound of a burial site, the contours of a Bronze Age village... a means of calling up the ghosts of the land's lost inhabitants...

– Jem Poster

The Fluent Stream

RUTH FAINLIGHT

Carol Ann Duffy, *The Bees*, Picador, £14.99, 9780330442442

Does Carol Ann Duffy keep bees? She knows a lot about them, and has chosen the bee as the emblem of her new book because without bees to pollinate them, there would be no trees, plants, flowers, fruit, vegetables. Which means that there would be no food, nothing for animals, including us, to eat. The bees' dance initiates the chain of life – they connect everything: "bees / are the batteries of orchards, garden, guard them" ('Virgil's Bees'). Bees represent order, productivity, visual and aural harmony. The buzz of a hive is like the sound of a place of worship where prayers are murmured and hummed. A hive of buzzing bees symbolises language, is language, and every separate bee is a word, "brazen, blurs on paper, / besotted; buzzwords [...] ", as she writes in the opening and title poem of this handsome book.

But the present state of our planet is febrile, precarious; Duffy is very aware of how human activity threatens all life forms. In 'The Woman in the Moon' ("How could you think it a man up here?"), the moon gazes down on a ravaged, polluted Earth – "deserts where forests were, sick seas" – at what human beings have done. Unlike most personifications of our satellite, Duffy's moon is an almost matronly figure, deeply maternal, appalled by what she witnesses but cannot control. Ecology (I suppose you could call it that, this protective yet stern awareness of what is happening all around us) is one of her subjects.

Duffy turns the same tender yet entirely unillusioned attention to many other subjects: family and friends, alive or dead; England; war. She is very good at writing about men and soldiers without the screen of classical distancing. 'The Falling Soldier', a description of the last moment of life for a fighter in the Spanish Civil War, is as vivid and disturbing an image in words as Robert Capa's great photograph is a visual one. (Beckham, in 'Achilles', merits the classical reference.) 'Last Post' marks the deaths of two of the last three surviving veterans of the First World War: 111-year-old Harry Patch and 113-year-old Henry Allingham. The poem, which Duffy read on BBC Radio 4's *Today* programme on the date of Allingham's funeral, has as its epigraph two lines from Wilfred Owen's poem 'Dulce et Decorum Est', and she quotes the words of his title with the same indignation as his, specifically to deny their message. (In 1913, the complete line, Horace's "Dulce et decorum est pro patria mori", was inscribed on the wall of the chapel of the Royal Military Academy Sandhurst. Frightful portent.) Owen's description of wounded survivors of a gas attack is horrifying, yet Duffy's poem is full of movingly positive images of the lives those dead soldiers should have lived.

I enjoy her obvious affection for things British, landscape and people and traditions; how she relishes the glorious sounds of proper names and place names ('The English Elms', 'The Counties', 'The White Horses'); and her grand celebrations of beer ('John Barleycorn', with its incantatory list of pub names) and of whisky ('Drams' – even though one stanza mourns: "The sad flit from here / to English soil, English air, / from whisky to beer"). She is ideally suited to the role of public poet as well as being a fine lyric one – a wonderful combination for a Poet Laureate.

The most deeply personal and tender of all are the poems about her daughter and her mother. When I first read 'Orta St Giulio' in the *TLS* last year, it produced that shiver at the back of the neck one feels encountering genuine poetry. It is exquisite: the twilit lake surrounded by mountains and clouds, the beautiful young girl standing there, watched by her mother, the poet who writes: "I slip behind her into the future; memory" – and then the final couplet: "A bat swoops, the lake a silence of dark light; / how it will be, must be."

The first line of 'Water' is: "Your last word was water"; the last line ends with the word "daughter". With immense skill, Duffy combines so many different times and memories into this elegy for her mother: the childhood memory of calling out for a drink and having her mother bring one and then sit on the edge of her bed and hold her hand in the dark; the vital presence of her own half-sleeping child calling out for a drink: "Water. / What a mother brings / through darkness still / to her parched daughter"; and how, after giving her mother that flimsy plastic hospice glass from which she took just one small sip, Duffy fell asleep in the chair next to the bed, then came awake with a jerk three hours later and gulped down the rest of the water in the glass – fortunate enough to be in time to hold her mother's hand until she died. This is a poem which is so achieved that at a first reading it might seem almost artless – but the more carefully you examine it the more you realise how well it demonstrates the total ease with which Duffy swims in what she terms "this fluent, glittery stream" of poetry.

Ruth Fainlight's most recent publication is *New & Collected Poems* (Bloodaxe, 2010).

Blod & Gots

AHREN WARNER

Simon Armitage, *The Death of King Arthur*,
Faber, £12.99, ISBN 9780571249473.

Simon Armitage's *The Death of King Arthur* is a contemporary rendering
of the four-thousand line, Middle English *Morte Arthure*. The original
poem – by an unknown poet of the North or Northeast Midlands, but
copied down by a Yorkshireman – is preserved in the Lincoln Thornton
Manuscript, which dates from the 1440s.

The Death of King Arthur follows the success of Armitage's translation of
Sir Gawain and the Green Knight (another Middle English poem in alliterative
verse) and begins with the story of the eponymous hero's European campaign
and eventual victory against the Roman Emperor Lucius (who provokes
Arthur by dispatching a fairly tetchy senator to demand "fealty"). The latter
part of the poem is dedicated to Arthur's death at the hands of the
treacherous Mordred, the knight Arthur had left in charge of Britain while he
fought on the continent.

There is much to recommend in Armitage's version of *Morte Arthure*, not
least the sheer energy he imbues into his alliterative lines. Technically, this is
not a meagre accomplishment; by rendering the original, pseudo-inflected
language into contemporary English, Armitage has had to find ways to
counteract the slowing of the line that the inevitably increased syllable count
of a non-inflected language brings with it, a feat he manages with panache in
the following lines:

> [...] the bold bowmen of Britain
> fought with foot-soldiers of foreign lands;
> their well-fletched arrows flew at the foe,
> piercing fine mail as far as the feathers.
> Such fighting did fearful harm to the flesh,
> and arrows flashed from afar into the flanks of the steeds.

Beyond Armitage's formal dexterity, he has constructed a poem that abounds
with vigour and humour, that engages and seduces the reader into something
akin to a "ripping yarn". Armitage also deserves credit for maintaining a

fidelity to the original text that other attempts to render the poem into contemporary English have been unable to muster. For example, a notable passage of the original text (lines 2483–2492) begins:

> The king calles on Florent,   that flowr was of knightes:
> "The Fraunchmen enfeebleshes;   ne ferly mē thinkes!
> They are unfonded folk   in tho fair marches,   ̄
> For them wantes the flesh   and food that them likes [...]"

These lines – cited from Benson's scholarly edition *King Arthur's Death* – and the subsequent seven, constitute an extended alliteration of the same consonant ("f") and, indeed, are a textual peculiarity of the original. In other renderings of *Morte Arthure*, such as Brian Stone's well-known version, the translator fails to fully carry this prolonged alliterative movement into the contemporary text. In contrast, Armitage manages it with gusto:

> the King called to Florent, that flower among knights:
> "Our Frenchmen are enfeebled, I should have guessed this would follow,
> for these folk are foreigners in these far-flung fields
> and long for the food and fare of their liking."

Yet, I would be uncomfortable with describing *The Death of King Arthur* as a wholly successful translation of *Morte Arthure*. If generations of great writers have warned us about the dangers of translation – from Voltaire ("malheur aux faiseurs de traductions littérales, qui, traduisant chaque parole, énervent le sens!" – *Lettres philosophiques*) through to Frost ("Poetry is what gets left out in translation") – one can only hope that the risk of such an undertaking is, at the very least, worth the pay-off.

In this context, the problem with Armitage's translation is simply that the pay-off is too limited. Given a scholarly edition that includes a good gloss, the reader who understands Armitage will also understand the original, which is fairly easy to read and enjoy. Furthermore, the very act of translating the alliterative line into a contemporary register that is foreign to it inevitably foregrounds its artifice.

> And Sir Gawain the good   in his gay armes,
> Umbegripped the gers   and on grouf fallen,
> His banners braiden down,   bęten of gūles,
> His brand and his bręde shēld   all bloody berunnen.

> Was never our seemlich king sọ sọrrowful in herte,
> Ne that sank him sọ sad but that sight ọne.

This is one example where original lines that have grit, that breathe or rasp, often end up like the following, blandly cartoonish, lines from Armitage's version:

> and good Sir Gawain in his glinting gear,
> face down in the field, fists full of grass,
> his bold red banners brought to the floor,
> his sword and broad shield swimming with blood.
> Never was our Sovereign so saddened and sorrowful,
> or sunk in his spirits as he was at that sight.

Armitage is indubitably an important poet. In large part, this is because he is one of the very few *public* poets of his generation – in the lineage of MacNeice and Harrison – to have produced work of real worth. Yet, on this occasion, Armitage's handling of the "Matter Of Britain" (unlike, for example, his excellent *Killing Time*) is somewhat flat. For, enjoyable and deft as *The Death of King Arthur* undoubtedly is, I would hazard that one might read *Morte Arthure* with as much ease as – and a more rewarding enjoyment than – Armitage's updating of it.

Ahren Warner's first collection, *Confer*, was published by Bloodaxe in 2011. He has also published a pocket-book, *Re:*, with Donut Press.

Paths Of Resistance

BEN WILKINSON

John Kinsella, *Armour*, Picador, £9.99, ISBN 9780330511841;
Timothy Donnelly, *The Cloud Corporation*, Picador, £9.99,
ISBN 9781447200420

"Poetry, perhaps more than any other literary form", claimed the critic G.J. Finch, "expresses the desire and need to be at home in the universe." If this statement seems too vague, or even grandiloquent, to repay real attention, think on the fullest sense of the etymology of "poet" as *maker* (from the Greek *poiētēs*: one who creates). Poetry serves to reimagine and ultimately remake the world around us. The good poet is aware of the anthropocentric perspective we bring to bear on everything, and good poems often deal – through the transformative power of language – with that gulf between the way our senses process the world, and the abundance and possibility of the universe beyond our human perception. Thus poetry jolts us from the trance of routine and function and, at its best, brings shifty reality into sharper relief, broadening our understanding of the universe, and how we fit into it.

Australian poet John Kinsella's new collection, *Armour*, often seeks to engage with the environment in these terms. At first glance a superabundant book of some sixty-odd poems, it unfolds into an atmospheric, intellectually persuasive *cri de coeur*; a poetic thesis of interrelated pieces that imaginatively negotiate the natural world's mysteries. These range from the scientifically unfathomable 'Sleep of Blowflies' to which "no / forensic kit gives clues", to the "armour" of the rhinoceros in 'Zoo Visits'. This "armour" lends the collection its title, but the thick skin and protection we all require can also be potentially restrictive: elsewhere Kinsella remembers Albrecht Dürer's sixteenth century woodcut of the creature with "metal breastplates and cuisses".

Rejecting the loaded label of "nature poet", Kinsella has said that he considers himself "a writer of the environment – an ethically and politically motivated writer who perceives each poem, each text I write, as part of a resistance against environmental damage." *Armour* evinces this: in winding poems of extended conceits that inhabit their subject matters uncannily ("a bristling queue" of 'Processional Caterpillars Mistaken for Spitfires'); in meditative sequences that quest and question while merging the mythical and modern (the fabled Aboriginal "Wagyl" of 'Idyllatry', a snakelike creator of waterways, found "in retreat as the river grows / more and more saline"); and in formal pieces that blend musical patterns with their ecological themes, such as the nightscape of 'Holus-Bolus', made alien by taut rhythms and incantatory end-rhymes:

> Mistletoe hang-dog meteorite,
> burn up with blue butterflies bright
> as all get up, or snakes and blue-
> tongues out and about, so too
>
> flyers too quick to identify. Risible.
> Goose-egg nest of oats, stressed oval
> mowed over without breaking,
> not a crack though black veins aching
>
> against the china-white.

Beyond *Armour*'s inventive reach and at times metaphysical cast of mind, however, is the sharp voice of protest. This is commendable, for sure – the target is always ignorance, head-burying, or anthropocentric blinkeredness – but when certain poems brandish Kinsella's politics (pacifist, anarchist, anti-capitalist) too readily, they not only risk overwhelming their more delicately convincing effects, but also alienating the reader. The throwaway establishment-bashing of the vignette 'Wirangu Meeting Place / Barton Siding' is fine in its context, a stirring closing sequence of sketches from a train journey across Western and South Australia. But a poem such as 'Habitat', which implicates the reader as one who "stares straight through", making crass assumptions about the world around them, far from curries favour. Better when, instead of getting mad, Kinsella gets even: couching the rural work of 'Hay Cutting' in the pervasive language of economics; "if the markets collapse / he'll still cut hay, and store / it for longer."

In many ways, *Armour* is a fittingly tough book. Its stylistic and tonal fecundity, resistant to the casual dip, demand that it be read cover to cover. For the reader who does so, its poems extend to offer ample rewards; a sturdy intellectual exterior gives way to revelation, memorably intense description, and – amid its spiky socio-political critiques – depth of feeling.

New Yorker Timothy Donnelly shares with Kinsella a whip-smart intelligence and environmental engagement. However, rather than reconnecting with flora, fauna and *terra firma*, Donnelly's poetry engages with the socially atomised, hyper-real, consumer-capitalist dream-cum-nightmare we have conjured for ourselves. 'To His Debt' is one of several poems in *The Cloud Corporation*, Donnelly's capacious second collection, that exercises a familiar delight in addressing an abstraction (think of Yeats's 'To a Shade' or, more recently, Nick Laird's *To a Fault*). But the unusually direct, sardonic wit masks pure frustration, pure contempt:

> Where would I be without you, massive shadow
> dressed in numbers, when without you there
>
> behind me, I wouldn't be myself. What wealth
> could ever offer loyalty like yours, my measurement,
>
> my history, my backdrop against which every
> coffee and kerplunk, when all the giddy whoring
>
> around abroad and after the more money money
> wants is among the first things you prevent.

Donnelly satirises a grimly recognisable world where money is god: as false an idol as Cortés was for the Aztecs, found here in 'Montezuma to his Magicians' with his fellow Conquistadors, leaping "upon the gold as dazzled / monkeys might". Such hall-of-mirrors complexities come under wicked scrutiny throughout the collection – from global economics to data overload to postmodern hesitancy, the all-pervasive clouds of the title sequence parting to reveal "the advocates of clouds, / believers in people, ideas and things". Yet Donnelly cajoles and tempers his anger, achieving a breezy, conversational and amused tone. The result is a high-proof cocktail mixed from the tercets of Wallace Stevens, a double shot of Whitman, and a twist of Ginsberg's 'Howl':

> I don't want to have to. I don't want to have to
> locate divinity in a loaf of bread, in a sparkler,
> or in the rainlike sound the wind makes through
>
> mulberry trees, not tonight. Listen to them carry on
> about gentleness when it's inconceivable
> that any kind or amount of it will ever be able to

balance the scales. I have been held down
by the throat and terrified, numb enough to know.
The temperature at which no bird can thrive [...]   ('The New Hymns')

A giddy mix, even an acquired taste, but Donnelly is rarely drunk on his looping, discursive style. Vignettes such as 'Chapter for Kindling a Torch' – *ars poetica* rendered as aphorism – suggest a trustworthy sensibility: Donnelly is aware when to hit the gas, and when to apply the brakes. This is writing of playful surrealism, serious philosophical depth, unshowy forms and disarming casualness. It deserves a wide audience, one hungry for a loquacious poetry of the here-and-now that uncovers wisdom, while – as in 'To His Detriment' – "never wearing me down entirely".

Ben Wilkinson is a poet, critic and PhD research student at Sheffield Hallam University.

A Clearinghouse
For Dreams And Visions

DAVID MORLEY

Charles Simic, *Dime-Store Alchemy: The Art of Joseph Cornell*,
NYRB Classics / Frances Lincoln, £9.99, ISBN 9781590174869;
Robert Crawford, *Simonides*, with photographs by Norman McBeath,
Easel Press, £35, ISBN 9780955285936;
Paul Munden, *Asterisk*: Poems & Photographs from Shandy Hall*, with
photographs by Marion Frith, Smith/Doorstop, £12.95, ISBN 9781906613334

"All art is a magic operation," writes Charles Simic, "or, if you prefer, a prayer for a new image". *Dime-Store Alchemy* (published in the USA a decade ago) is a series of remarkable ecphrastic reflections on the art and life of Joseph Cornell in which Cornell's boxes of magic junk are presented together with Simic's enigmatic writing. The poet's responses are chiefly reflections on the philosophy and process of making, presented as prose poetry:

Cornell's boxes are like witch doctors' concoctions.
They contain objects that have sacred and magical
properties. The box is a little voodoo temple with an altar.
Love medicine or medicine of immortality is being prepared.

('Vaudeville de Luxe')

Dime-Store Alchemy is both an account of the mystery of making, and a fractured biography of a maverick and wonderful artist. The American surrealist Joseph Cornell was born on the Hudson River in 1903. As a young man, he fossicked in second-hand bookshops and junk stores, collecting discarded books, records, photographs, prints, theatrical memorabilia and prints of old movies. In 1931 Cornell discovered the Julien Levy gallery, and watched the owner unpack the surrealist objects and paintings sent over from France. Inspired by their precise arbitrariness and deft execution, Cornell investigated his trove of discovered junk to create two-dimensional montages. Levy admired them and encouraged the youthful avant-gardist to intrigue him further. Simic evokes the process:

Here's how Cornell described the contents of some
150 files he kept at home:

a diary journal repository laboratory, picture
gallery, museum, sanctuary, observatory, key...
the core of a labyrinth, a clearinghouse for dreams
and visions... childhood regained.

('Dog Wearing Baby Clothes')

Cornell tried out various physical framing devices for his montages, designing boxes (Simic calls them "oneiric playhouses") in which to array his materials, repeating and varying certain images serially. Cornell went on to make films using cinema collages of spliced old film: "If you love watching movies from the middle on, Cornell is your director," writes Simic. Marcel Duchamp became an admirer. Cornell's fame grew strongly after his work featured in the Museum of Modern Art's 1936 exhibition 'Fantastic Art, Dada, Surrealism'. All this detail, yet as Simic writes in 'Emily Dickinson':

Cornell and Dickinson are both in the end
unknowable. They live within the riddle, as
Dickinson would say. Their biographies explain

nothing. They are without precedent, eccentric, original, and thoroughly American. If her poems are like his boxes, a place where secrets are kept, his boxes are like her poems, the place of unlikely things coming together.

You can see why Charles Simic would find himself gravitating to Joseph Cornell's alert, enclosed surrealism. Simic's poetry possesses a parallel perceptual edginess and a sense for private obsessiveness *pace* Dickinson (qualities that can be said to apply to all three books under review). Similarly, both Cornell and Simic have made art that is immediately vivid and likeable at some level while never being obvious. Both artists make clear mysteries of the world around them in all its trashiness and irregularity. Charles Simic's miniaturist boxes of speech and prose poetry are as charming and as strange as Joseph Cornell's boxes of shape, shadow and silence.

When Horace wrote that poetry is like a painting he could never have foreseen the three-headed work that is *Simonides*. Simonides is of course the name of an ancient Greek poet known for his terse epitaphs and work on memory. This book is a collaboration between the poet Robert Crawford and the acclaimed photographer Norman McBeath (who has also worked with other contemporary writers including Jeanette Winterson, A. L. Kennedy, Janice Galloway and Paul Muldoon). The project pairs Scots (and English) versions of ancient Greek epitaphs with contemporary black and white photographs. Stark images collide with pithy texts, supporting one another, while Scots renderings surprise and subvert the subject matter. The themes largely revolve around the War on Terror (the book contains an excellent essay by Robert Crawford, "Simonides and the War on Terror").

The shade of Ian Hamilton Finlay and Little Sparta ('Terror is the Piety of the Revolution') falls generously and bracingly over this work. A photo of the curving internal woodwork of a boat faces an epitaph called 'Waves':

> The nummer o the swaws...
>
> The number of the waves...

I am delighted to see some of Finlay's aesthetic challenges being taken up by Robert Crawford. No writer has seriously picked up on Finlay's minimalist texts on revolution or war. When Finlay wrote that poetry can exist through a single word or "detached sentence" he intended to create a resonant but ordered simplicity. Crawford manages both to take on these challenges and to take them further through his versions of Simonides. Norman McBeath's eerie photograph of a galvanised cattle trough is almost completely outfaced by the epitaph 'Lair' (and its companion version in synthetic Scots):

> Frien, this is nae grand laird's mausoleum.
> A puir man needs nae big lair. This'll dae.

> Friend, this is no great lord's tomb. A poor man
> does not require a big tomb. This one will do.

The precision of Crawford's essay also embraces the Spartan style. "The greatest poems of the ancient Greek poet Simonides", it opens, "are body bags". Robert Crawford's work in *Simonides* is profound, provocative and magnificently grim.

As an act of cultural ecphrasis Paul Munden's *Asterisk** is a complex but light-footed salvaging of found poetry, sculpture, film, criticism, biography, natural history, autobiography, historical commentary, architectural appreciation, and real and imagined stories. At face value, the book is a sequence of poems by Munden inspired by Shandy Hall, the extraordinary house in Coxwold that was once home to the writer Laurence Sterne. The book is "a personal interpretation of things Shandean" combined with very fine photographs of the house and garden by Marion Frith who works at the Hall. Beyond face value, the book is created and collaged through and from such multi-faceted and varied sources that the project as a whole is tentative, open-ended and delightfully riddling. Like *Tristram Shandy*, the book disarms the reader with mischievousness, candour and humour:

> Grenada was *Omeros*; Portugal, *To the Hermitage*.
> The south of France was *Don Quixote*
> in the baking heat of the beach
> outside the walls of the Chateau de La Napoule.

> I wandered from my book into the castle gardens,
> a parallel world of cool walkways and fountains
> where the madcap knight himself accosted me
> in his naked copper-green. But to return –

> *Tristram Shandy* was a corner of Umbria,
> seven children making mayhem in the pool,

bonding with a summer's dimpled pleasures
before finding new horizons of their own.

Some of the most successful and effective ecphrastic poems involve and
include the writer of the poems. Poetry about Laurence Sterne's house and
"things Shandean" might have proved wilfully designed had not Paul
Munden placed himself playfully within the poems. The centre of attention
in *Asterisk** is twofold, and the autobiographical focus and force of the
poetry are what balance and ignite the project, making the whole of the work
elliptically alive.

David Morley's next collection of poetry, *World's Eye*, is due from Carcanet next year. He is
Professor of Writing at Warwick University.

Trajectories In Time

HILARY DAVIES

Kevin Crossley-Holland, *The Mountains of Norfolk, New and Selected Poems*,
Enitharmon Press, £10.99, ISBN 9781907587108;
Lotte Kramer, *New and Collected Poems*, Rockingham Press, £9.99,
ISBN 9781904851431

The literary parabolas these two writers have traced are indicative of
the diverse nature of contemporary British poetry: Kevin Crossley-
Holland's lifetime engagement with not only poetry but also
childrens' literature, translation, playwriting, broadcasting, editing, libretti
composition and teaching; and Lotte Kramer's evolution from Kindertransport
German speaker to late first publication at the age of fifty-five. These
collections are instructive of how each has engaged with language.

For Crossley-Holland, the mountains of Norfolk are not ironic, but real.
The eponymous poem is a rather overwritten celebration of sugarbeet, an
unsung mainstay of the north Norfolk economy, but other, imaginative,
mountains are everywhere in this collection. East Anglia is that liminal place

where land, sea and sky war with and fertilise each other. It is there from the earliest poems, "I only guess where marsh / finishes and sky begins" ('Dusk, Burnham-Overy-Staithe') to the most recent, "The welter; the rim; / the colours of separation; / always the ache of his tides / chiming/deep within." ('Moored Man's Tides'). Crossley-Holland has so breathed these creeks and marshes, touched them, smelt them, eaten from them, that "Moored Man" can rise out of the mud and slime like Poseidon, or a lungfish, or an ancient mariner. The metaphor is justified, alive. Moreover, Crossley-Holland knows that craft and art are indivisible when it comes to poetry. His evocations work because he has taken care to shape what he wants to say: the best poems are held together by unforced rhyme, assonance, alliteration, a careful sense of form which lifts language to a level beyond the everyday, towards a state of perception that illuminates or redeems:

> Tilted my hat, down on all fours, stalking:
> Two deer high-tailed it, swerving and forking
> and criss-crossing.
> > Fireflies danced all that night.
> On one wrist I wore a bracelet of light.
> I dreamed the old dream: solve it by walking.
> > > ('Solvitur Ambulando')

Lotte Kramer's *New and Collected Poems* represents a life's work, all the more noteworthy in that it is in a language which, although she has lived in it since the age of fifteen, is nevertheless not her mother tongue. This is a hard art to master but, with a linguistic modesty that characterises the whole volume, she achieves it. The range of her subject matter covers, as one might expect, the gamut encountered in a long life: childhood, marriage, motherhood, old age, as well as the intellectual enjoyment taken in painting and music. But Lotte Kramer's experience is not that of many of her English contemporaries, even those who lived through the Second World War. With remarkable delicacy she turns again and again to the source of her inspiration. It is of course that of flight from Nazi Germany, the loss of her family, the exile from language, home, security, and the welcome offered by strangers in a strange land:

> Myself, I'm unsure
> In both languages. One, with mothering
> Genes [...]

> The other, a constant love affair
> Still unfulfilled, a warm
> Shoulder to touch.   ('Bilingual')

Kramer is never guilty of sleeve-tugging: her very understatement makes what she says more telling, as in the excellent sonnet sequence, 'Post-War'. Two members of her family come out of Germany alive after the war, their experiences dwarfing her own difficulties:

> They'd walked on quicksand through a human lie.
> [...] Our lives could not compare
> With those dark memories that they could not share. ('Post-War IV')

Elsewhere the poem 'Judgement' stands as both warning and corrective to the injudicious arrogation of another's suffering by writers less scrupulous than herself, "You who have not walked / Through the blurred edges of my Hades, / [...] Do not encapsulate /A judgement or eavesdrop on pain." Kramer knows how to make an object or anecdote carry cultural or historical weight: the Rhine is a constant companion but also a cruel reminder right through the collection, "Sand in my blood / Edging the Rhine's centuries, / My life's river / Kneeling at the town's cobbles, / Watering / The reddening sins" ('Journey'). It is true to say that at three hundred and ninety-eight pages some editorial pruning would have been useful, and there is evidence from the surprising number of typos – one poem even unforgivably divorced from its title – that production was rushed. Nevertheless, Rockingham Press has done the reading public good service by making this corpus of work more generally available: Lotte Kramer stands as a witness both to and against the worst that humanity can do. Her message is one to which we should all pay heed.

Hilary Davies's *Imperium* is published by Enitharmon.

Adaptations And Adjustments

ALAN BROWNJOHN

Derek Mahon, *Raw Material*, Gallery Press, £10.50, ISBN 9781852355234;
Eiléan Ní Chuilleanáin, *Legend of the Walled-up Wife: translations from the Romanian of Ileana Mălăncioiu*, Gallery Press, £10.50, ISBN 9781852355197

The Author's Note at the beginning of this collection of translations by Derek Mahon of a wide variety of poets, classic, or simply dead, or still very much alive, is short; which is wise. Attempting at greater length to define exactly what he has done with the work of Sextus Propertius, or three eighth century Chinese poets, or Rimbaud, or Neruda, or Michel Houellebecq would have plunged the distinguished Ulster poet into a maze where everyone else is angrily eager to tell you the way out. Mahon merely quotes, so as to disagree with him, Ted Hughes advocating "the very oddity and struggling dumbness of a word for word version"; otherwise, "the value of the whole enterprise is called into question." He could have cited on his own side Robert Lowell calling his 1962 book *Imitations*; or the innumerable poets and drama translators who have taken liberties with that word "version"; or others who have tried "variations".

One of the best ever contributions to this debate, in the form of an excellent metaphor, was made by theatre director Michael Meyer (what would he have thought of Mahon's rendering of Ibsen?) who said that translation should offer a clear window onto a landscape which the glass of a foreign language prevented you from entering; he greatly disliked modernisation of texts. But Lowell's settling for "one voice running through many personalities, contrasts and repetitions" is what most poet-translators seem to have gone along with. Mahon calls his own efforts "adaptations", and his is a vigorous modern voice.

It is quickly clear that he has worked his way thoroughly and sympathetically into the spirit of the classical poems – one extract from Ovid and nine from Propertius – for a start. His accounts of the Propertius love poems are superbly racy, with only occasional concessions to modern colloquial usage, a common trap for translators; though Propertius's forthright Cynthia, returning to the poet in a dream after her death, might have reproached him for his neglect with more dignity than Mahon allows her:

you who were nowhere near me when I died—
stricken with grief, sez you. Cheat! Lying sod!
Had you been there you might have eased the pains
but no, you were too busy with your floozies [...]

The one Baudelaire poem is titled 'Antrim Road', which is presumably meant to suggest that suburban ennui is international because it originates in one of the French poet's 'Tableaux Parisiens', ("Je n'ai pas oublié, voisine de la ville, / Notre blanche maison"). Here, Baudelaire's evening sun appears to be "silently watching mushy peas and spuds", which rather lowers the romantic tone of "Semblait [...] / Contempler nos diners longs et silencieux." Rimbaud's 'Ma Bohème' (which becomes 'Hitchhiker') suffers in a different but related way, from too much modernisation of references. Nothing dates as much as updating, and the naive charm of "Stargazing Tom Thumb, I sowed rhymes along the way" (to translate the Baudelaire literally) is lost with Mahon's "Roaming under the heavens I scattered pearls / of poetry, a rock star in my dreams." Another Rimbaud poem is 'Cupboard' ('Le Buffet'), which is both loyal to the original and venturesome in Mahon's adaptation. In French it begins "C'est un large buffet sculpté; le chêne sombre, / Tres vieux [...]." But let Mahon take over and continue, and we have:

Unlock this great old cupboard of carved oak
and it gives out intriguing intimations
like a wine-bin chock-full of vintage wines;
the wood has the fine grain of ancient folk.

There are similar pleasures in his translations of Rilke, Jorge Guillén and Pablo Neruda, but it's hard to assess what he has achieved with the Chinese poets, worked on with the aid of a Chinese scholar, or with what appear to be versions of works by African poets writing in French. Which raises another matter: the book is not really reader-helpful. A few originals facing the translations would have been good to have (except perhaps for the Chinese and Indian poems; it would have been expensive, and for the Indian impossible, for reasons soon to be disclosed), and so would some information about the poets themselves and how Mahon came to make translations of the living ones. Presumably he didn't work with the Africans (from where?) or the Haitian? In the end there is an air of randomness about the collection, though that doesn't diminish its interest. Yet also: the title of the book is the title of the long translation with which it ends, "from the

Hindi of Gopal Singh ('born 1959')", a sequence set in a modern India of poverty and disaster, riches and recycling which reads as well as all the others in Mahon's "one voice running through many personalities". But Mr Singh, he reveals, is "my own invention" as a tribute to real Indian poems. It makes the book seem rather a mixture; at seventy-seven pages it doesn't carry the weight of Robert Lowell's *Imitations*, which ran to one hundred and forty five pages in paperback. One can only hope Mahon goes on extending the range of his "adaptations".

In her generous selection from the poems of Ileana Mălăncioiu, with whom she has worked to produce this book, the Irish poet Eiléan Ní Chuilleanáin has resolutely allowed the Romanian – arguably her country's finest living poet – to retain, as far as possible, her own register. There are no wilful colloquialisms, only a few adjustments to suit "an ordinary Irish speaking voice". Ní Chuilleanáin's choice was ample: Mălăncioiu, who has published over twenty books, has from the beginning been a prolific writer of terse and powerful short poems reflecting her rural upbringing (its myths, legends and terrors: ghosts, assassins, a giant with huge iron hands and fourteen nostrils) and then, in the late years of the Ceauşescu regime, showing a change of emphasis by taking up social and political subjects. These were mostly hidden in fable, but detectable enough for the censors to require changes to the content of one notable volume in 1985. Love and death have been constant themes of her macabre, romantic poems, and never treated conventionally. In 'Song of Joy' the gladness of the lovers is both equivocal in itself and under external threat; the gifts passing between them are surreally meagre ("sparrow's eggs" and "cuckoo's milk"), the roof of their home houses a hawk's nest. 'Custom' imagines a ceremony of disinterring the dead so as to mourn them again; and then "leave them back in the graves they had before / And lay on top of them a firmer stone".

It would be wrong to see too many of the mysterious, sometimes violent, occasionally erotic poems of this period as some kind of political rebellion (though 'A Crime' and 'Just That' are unquestionably so). Mălăncioiu is a rebel against the mercilessness of life itself, its betrayals and bereavements, its casual indifference to its endemic cruelties – see the harrowing title poem, or 'Cheerful Songs': "When death began to cut down / Somebody every day / You all went on singing party pieces." In 'Game' her only solution is to keep playing it, with fatalistic persistence: "What else can I do, / I will answer. // Then silently / I will continue moving! Stone after stone, / Mountain after mountain." Eiléan Ní Chuilleanáin has honoured these dark and painful yet passionate and resonant poems with beautifully lucid and gripping translations.

Alan Brownjohn's latest book is *The Saner Places: Selected Poems* (Enitharmon, 2011).

Being Human

STEVEN MATTHEWS

Mimi Khalvati, *Child: New and Selected Poems 1991-2011*,
Carcanet, £12.95 ISBN 9781847770943;
Stanley Moss, *God Breaketh Not All Men's Hearts Alike: New and Later
Collected Poems*, Seven Stories Press, £24.36, ISBN 9781609803452

These two books offer telling variations upon the problem of constructing a narrative from a life. Mimi Khalvati garners a freshness to her selections from five previous volumes by structuring *Child* around a progression: from childhood to motherhood, to poems considering light, then to the connections between love and art. The book ends by circling back to beginnings. Stanley Moss, from the serene and seemingly joyful plateau of age, has work looking back down through the years at the experiences, odd events and encounters, which have brought him to where he has now arrived. Both poets mount important celebrations of their lives, the contexts which their former selves relished, and the assurances (technical, authorial) which growing maturity has brought.

Khalvati's work has always operated out of the measuring of distances; it records the losses and advantages of being brought up between two worlds, Tehran and seaside England, and of the disturbance of being on the move. Her most consistent and innovative poems embrace that displacement as a given, and take their angles and perspectives upon it. The extended sequence 'Interiors' about the painter Edouard Vuillard, for instance, figures studies of a workroom in which both art and dresses are produced, "the sensation of the eye / from the highest corner of the room" in which childhood, "like a fishspine between sun and moon [...] luxuriates!" The paradox, as in much of Khalvati's poetry, is that a concluding envisaged fullness (here that of childhood) is arrived at through a complex set of vocal manoeuvrings and syntactic shiftings. The negative aspect of this manoeuvring is that some of the poems' endings, when arrived at, come with a degree of melodrama, even when self-parodic – "luxuriates!"

Given this, and after rereading Khalvati's work as a whole, the poems that remain most strongly in the memory are those in which traditional form is allowed to contain much of this organisational business. The ghazals offer their particular cumulative strengths, but the sonnets and sonnet sequences, rhymed and unrhymed, pace the voice compellingly. In that sense, the sequence 'Love in an English August' stands out as a brilliantly generous encapsulation of the fears and hopes of a relationship; 'The Meanest Flower' sequence is different again, in its rendition of the travails of childhood. By comparison to these achievements, some of the new work included here feels purposeless. A loose gathering of sketches as 'Iowa Daybook' tries to make a virtue of this. The Belgium-set 'The Streets of La Roue', however, offers an intriguing new tack, its unrhymed sonnets seeking both to contain the mess of the everyday, while also asking for a philosophical or political means to bring it all back into order: "I am looking for a guiding spirit, / where will I find it, *chez vous, chez vous, / chez eux?*" That "spirit" emerges as Erasmus, whose "adages" offer a jaded, "rusted" but benign civil proscription: "UBI BENE, / IBI PATRIA." Earlier poems had self-consciously concluded by lauding reciprocity, as in 'River Sonnet' – "sky thinking itself / in river, river thinking itself in sky." There are hints, in the new work gathered in *Child*, that Khalvati's perennial themes of distance and strangeness are taking a new suggestion to exciting limits in their consideration of potential national reconciliation, even though it is one in which distance and difference are benignly accommodated.

The voluble Stanley Moss, even when operating in formal constraint, seems to relish the messiness and concomitant provocativeness offered by a variety of poses in relation to a welter of experiences. This playing it on the edge finds its cheeky zenith, perhaps, in the many tauntings of Yahweh presented in this later collected work:

> [...] You are the Judge
> and I the guilty. Who should have mercy
> on the guilty if not the judge? You are All
> and I am a particle. Who should have mercy
> on a particle if not the All?

And so it continues, sometimes with hilarious results. If Moss seems wrong-headed in his eager embrace of the persona of modern satyr, as he does at several points here (the book ends with said satyr's prose "diary"), his relish for the joys which the everyday world offers, in nature or among humanity, is often irresistible. The brief poem 'Then' is typical, in its discovery of such delight in the most unlikely situation. As always, the poem begins with a contention: "In our graves we become / children again". But the development of the theme moves, also typically, towards the high but simple notes of celebration, as in death "we" become "birds to sing / songs without words / mating calls [...] / that call the day is glorious."

Moss's poems are honest about the ways in which habit, longevity, illness-threatening death, can all take their speakers inward, away from the surrounding reality in its "glory". They serve as constant reminders to turn back outwards, to look up. As 'Heart Work', about a recent operation, contends, it is still possible to hear Mozart, to see geese flying along a river on the same day as surgery: "I had forgotten the beauty in the world. / I remember. I remember." These poems are striking in their ready appropriation of the Whitman tradition in American poetry: they take up the challenge to encapsulate the multitudinousness of the world, but also measure the scariness of what the world has become. 'Subway Token' considers the earlier poet's possible responses to the events of 9/11, and acknowledges the inadequacy of all response, including that of poetry – "What history, what hallucination?" The poem ends by acknowledging, in a fiercely nationalistic vision, the failure of literature to measure up to the enormity, as "You could not pile books so high, not good books, / as this grand canyon of steel and concrete body parts", the former World Trade Center.

Whatever our unease with some of these provocations ("grand canyon"!), Moss's poetry offers good, and often enlivening, talk; wherever it sets out from or arrives at, it takes us past unexpected and engaging places along the way.

Steven Matthews's collection of poems, *Skying*, is forthcoming from Waterloo Press.

Lyrical, Experimental
And Colloquial

ALEX RUNCHMAN

Jules Supervielle, trans. Moniza Alvi, *Homesick For The Earth*,
Bloodaxe, £9.95, ISBN 9781852249205;
Marianne Boruch, *The Book of Hours*, Copper Canyon Press,
$15, ISBN 9781556593857;
Ian McMillan, *This Land Used to be Frozen: Lamps*,
Smith/Doorstop Books, £5, ISBN 9781906613402;
Jerome Rothenberg, *Retrievals: Uncollected & New Poems, 1955–2010*,
Junction Press, $21, ISBN 9781881523192;
Terry Jones, *Furious Resonance*, Poetry Salzburg Pamphlet Series,
£5, ISBN 9783901993350

T. S. Eliot regarded Jules Supervielle (1884–1960) as one of the poets of his generation whose work was most likely to stand the test of time. It's easy to see what Eliot might have valued in Supervielle's verse: the two poets engage with the same Symbolist heritage and share preoccupations with eyes and blindness, the sea, and memory. Supervielle is attracted to the universal – "la Terre"– and to the vastness of the Atlantic and the Andes. He is less concerned with local landscapes or individuals. "I drag along with me more than one living soul", he proclaims in 'Poet', while several poems are spoken in God's voice. 'La goutte de pluie' ('The Raindrop'), in which God fails to find a raindrop recently fallen in the sea, is imagistic in its simplicity, while 'Prophecy' and 'Homesick for the Earth' are anticipatory elegies written for the planet. Other poems sound a more explicitly conservationist strain; 'In the Forest', for example, implores birds in a future felled forest to build their nests "here / in this memory of height. Quickly, / while it is still murmuring."

Despite prophesying the Earth's ruin, Supervielle is less disillusioned than Eliot. He is also less intellectually ambitious, and his poems, despite formal variety, are more resonant collectively than individually – a further facet, perhaps, of his universality. Are these reasons why they have not been better remembered? Their most enduring quality is their lyricism. Moniza Alvi's sensitive versions – they are not literal translations – in this dual-text edition capture much of "the particular music of the French language". They can't always match the originals. Alvi's decision to shorten the lines of 'Prière à l'inconnu' ('Prayer to the Unknown') makes a much sparer poem, and in 'Plein Ciel' ('Open Sky'):

> It was a ship, not a horse,
> a longing rather than a ship.
> It was a horse I'd never seen

sounds prosaic against Supervielle's softer anaphoric repetitions:

> C'était un navire
> Plutôt qu'un cheval,
> C'était un désir
> Plutôt qu'un navire,
> C'était un cheval
> Comme on n'envoit pas

Mostly, however, Alvi's interpretations – of the shorter lyrics especially – are judicious, introducing English readers to a poet who deserves to be better known.

At the end of a poem which begins "The poem put on its hair shirt, four lines / To a stanza", Marianne Boruch wonders "What happens to a thought / come in quiet?", further suggesting that stanzas are "Little vast rooms of undoing". Each of the poems in *The Book of Hours* is hair-shirted; each accommodates thoughts that come in quiet, often unexpectedly, within a fixed form; and each seeks to make the little vast. Predominantly meditative in tone, the poems contain undifferentiated voices that contemplate religion, history, memory and nature. Many of them have an enigmatic, Dickinsonian quality, written in syntax that is simple and yet somehow strange:

> Leaf multiplies to tree to make
> shade finally. You forgot what you
> love about light is dark –

The poems are sometimes aphoristic: a bird feigning a broken wing prompts the realisation that "Fear hot-wired to hope / Is sacrifice", while, elsewhere, God warns a would-be saint that "Every gift / is a curse". The book's contemporary voices rest more uneasily. A soldier summarises his experience in Iraq: "Been there. Got the T-shirt, got the fairly / decent pepperoni (really hot dog) pizza / in the Green Zone." The resort to cliché isn't adequate to the task of lyricising real colloquial speech. Such moments unbalance an otherwise intricate collection that rewards multiple readings.

Writing poems colloquially is Ian McMillan's stock-in-trade. But this comes at a price. 'It's the 4th of July!' begins:

> Always, for me, the struggle
> Between populism and
> Linguistically interesting work

Few poets have done as much as McMillan to promote spoken word poetry, to suggest that "mak[ing] play with words" is not just for an elite. As one of his characters insists, "*Ah cud gut't theatre / If ah wanted, ah reckon*". This is Macmillan at his most authentic, employing his own Yorkshire dialect and celebrating the mundane. And yet, many of the poems in *This Lake Used to be Frozen: Lamps* lack verbal energy. On the page, the repetitions and bathetic humour that might carry a poem in performance are mere surface effects. Sometimes, as in 'The Idea of Loneliness in the Little Chef, Uttoxeter' (with its titular nod to Wallace Stevens), or 'Platform 2', the repetitions do succeed in creating a sense of stasis and melancholy. But one still comes away wishing that the poems were less genial and more "linguistically interesting".

Jerome Rothenberg, in contrast, never stops seeking new possibilities for language in poems written both for the page and performance. *Retrievals* recovers poems omitted from collections over the last half-century which reflect the poet's "feeling that poetry as [he] wanted or needed it should be inventing or changing forms of meaning & expression". This book contains baroque sonnets, conversations, "deep image" poems, exuberant language games and sparse ecphrastic poems in response to icons and altarpieces; its defining characteristics are formal and linguistic experimentation and playfulness. Some poems rely upon mantra-like repetitions, others contain lines – and sometimes stanzas – of a single word, and still others reformulate an initial statement, suggesting that there is no fixed text. Rothenberg notes the development of "a kind of proto-'language poetry'", but one linked "to specific themes & stances" – and it is his interest in Jewish history, literary heritage, contemporary art and the astrological, among other subjects, that helps to distinguish his work from the kind of language poetry that divorces language from meaning. The responses to other poets are among the most distinguished pieces here. 'The Pound Project' merges Pound's voice with Rothenberg's own, while 'Fifteen for Haroldo' takes translations from the

Brazilian poet Haroldo De Campos and echoes them mimetically:

> *burnt by*
>> *asthma*
>
> churn'd
>> miasma
>
> .
>
> *a blind*
>> *nail*
>>> *oiling*
> *sun's*
>> *axis*
>
> a kind
>> whale
>>> spoiling
> nun's
>> praxis

As with any body of serious experimental poetry, there are misses as well as hits. 'A Poem of Fears', for example, all one hundred and seventy six lines of which begin "some had a fear of", becomes a tedious catalogue. But *Retrievals* provides more than enough evidence of what Charles Bernstein has called Rothenberg's "animating spirit".

Terry Jones's attraction to the fricatives and plosives of Anglo Saxon complements his eye for an apt image. Sprouting spuds are seen as "a row of cold knuckles'" and he tells us that one, rotting, "grew a halo of white hair". Another, "missed in the sack / was lifted out / the shrunken head of Medusa". In 'Sun', meanwhile, Jones seeks new epithets for "our common star": "Silverpisser seedchanger darkdrinker shiterotter / Leafblood eyeater deadmelter bonefixer". But he can be lyrical too, addressing it as "red ghost, horizon's flower, / bright reed, wish-scratch, alphabet, source". Although clever, such endeavours suggest more of the workshop exercise than of inspiration. A poem about burning a batch of dictionaries imagines language "alight / on a fuse running from word to word", but *Furious Resonance*, despite vivid visualisations and technical accomplishment, never quite ignites.

Alex Runchman teaches and lectures at Trinity College Dublin. He has recently completed a PhD on the American poet Delmore Schwartz.

Out Of Silence

DOUGLAS HOUSTON

Jacob Sam-La Rose, *Breaking Silence*, Bloodaxe, £8.95, ISBN 9781852249151;
Judy Brown, *Loudness*, Seren, £8.99, ISBN 9781854115478;
Tiffany Atkinson, *Catulla et al*, Bloodaxe, £8.95, ISBN 9781852248888

*B*reaking Silence traces Jacob Sam-La Rose's emergence from a speechlessness that is encoded on every level and becomes oppressive with adolescence:

> but I feel like an ink blot on a blank page and I know
> I'm not supposed to talk back. *No* is inked out from
> the lexicon of polite exchange between mother and son,
>
> and a friend says *it's best if you don't give it lip*
> *when they pick you up in the street*. If you're smart,
> you know when to stay silent. ('Speechless')

Numerous poems confront the reader with the experience of black youth on the South London streets, marginalised and finding refuge in the cultural autonomy of hip-hop and basketball. We get the inside story on black *attitude* as a pre-emptive tactic, a kind of mean cool for warding off encroachments on private space won from anger, discrimination and silence:

> Mostly, you're cool about it, but
> all the attention gets tired real quick –
> eyes peering in, eager to strip you back,
> layer by layer, until there's nothing left. ('How To Be Black')

'The Star' marks the violent end of that guarded identity with the shooting of a friend, an event which turns Sam-La Rose towards the freedoms language will open to him. The poem's emotional surge rides on the rhythmic and formal control that typically orders the wealth of imagery Sam-La Rose packs into his work. The opening's figuring of the star as wildcard symbol for language underwrites the visionary clarity of the ending's suburban panorama:

All that, before the walk back through Peckham Rye
where you picked out a single bright star
    shining above street-lamps, sirens
and the distant whine of a passing plane,
praising the blind tenacity of that
    single point of light.

The poems in which Sam-La Rose traces his quest for a voice and his subsequent mission to lead others out of "fierce and stubborn silence" ('Faith') encompass more than this brief review can make evident. The five parts of 'Speechless', for example, richly interweave modern history and personal background, while objectively detached poems like the account of domestic abuse in 'Reportage' broaden his work's interest and achievement.

Judy Brown begins *Loudness* with reflective poems on personal circumstances and day-to-day living, impressing with her talent for sharp imagery and tidy forms, but leaving the reader unprepared for the outbreak of strangeness in 'The Blackmailer's Wife Reads History And Considers The Nature Of Guilt'. Brown's lightness of touch in managing tone and imagery comes into its own in this poem, an imaginative drift anchored to evocations of the moon that charms with its opulent detail and easy manner while avoiding any hint of a context: "Arabesquing over my shoulder at the mirror, I see the Emperor Hirohito / smiling bluishly through the white skin of my arse. (Later a blank canvas.) / My husband says no: it was only mist passing over the security light."

From thereon in, the collection takes on an imaginative charge that sparks many surprises. One of several poems that sidestep cleanly any question as to whether they are exuberantly imagined or vividly factual is 'The Helicopter Visions', with the exhilarating sweep of its ten-minute flight over London. The ending adds an otherworldly twist – "above me the gods are strung / like fine chandeliers" – but not before the poem has landed safely on known ground: "All too soon we hang overhead, a thudding / barge of air, settle our weight into the slack, / the landing space. Even now it shakes me / when the crowded colours of earth strike the glass / as we're suddenly sucked down. We spill – / friction hot – into the morning at Willesden."

Brown writes with an unflappable detachment that focuses from a useful distance on whatever she chooses, be it getting the sack ('P45'), drunkenness ('Embittered, A Loner'), macro-economics ('The Crash'), or the candidly unsatisfactory erotic encounters that are equally written off against experience in various poems, most notably 'The Expats'. This is one of a group drawing on Brown's years in Hong Kong, poems dense with brilliantly lit images that register almost incidentally the expatriate's daily experience of being "amazed at novelties of a minor kind" ('Thirst'). There's no telling what Brown will do next, but it will be worth reading.

The re-gendered updates of Catullus that make up the first half of Tiffany Atkinson's collection stick to the spirit rather than the letter of the originals in giving us their essential themes, their knowing familiarity of address, and cultivated scurrility of tone while freely adapting particulars. 'Basia mille', for example, breathes the same reckless abandonment to love as "Vivamus, mea Lesbia" and its line of English imitations. Like all Atkinson's work here, the poem is also loyal to Catullus's lapidary style in its economies of diction and the carefully judged impact of its lines, for all the throwaway colloquialism that renders it firmly *de nos jours*:

> Let any fucker work us out
> who hasn't better business
>
> for their small hours. Meanwhile
> kiss me in the checkout queue
> and let the tight mouths clatter –
>
> scandal's for neurotics and they live
> on small change. Kiss me then, as
> daylight follows to the power of

'Basia mille' ends thus, falling, like others here, slightly short of closure to convey the hectic continuity of Catulla's life and times. Though seriousness never gets the better of her, there are moments when a primal darkness beyond the sex and gossip is palpable. For example, '00.52' broods with a chilling *ça ne fait rien* on suicide – "You might do worse than think about it, lady: / all you could let go".

'Et al', the collection's second part, shakes off the Catulla persona while retaining her acuteness of tone and recurrent concern with social and erotic experience. In 'Bad Karaoke' comic good nature triumphs over marital disaster: "dinna make me drive home on a hangover's / slipped gears   the sun on my forehead past / Dumfries   still asking why indeed   Delilah".

Occasional poems start conventionally enough in landscape or the weather and disclose their depths through tautness of style and singularly precise imagery. Others, notably 'Princess; Pea' and 'After Bluebeard', riskily balance captivating surfaces and dark narrative lacunae. Nothing is hidden, however, in 'According To', the final poem, which transports the reader to the simple heart of a remote Welsh rural community. With its biblical cadences and artful management of English as a seeming second language, the poem recalls Caradoc Evans's tales, although unlike these it takes a wholly optimistic view of human potential – "hopefuller than all the Born Again Virgins of America" – in ending with its vision of a world re-awoken and rebuilt. Elijah's message is broadly familiar, but, like Catullus, he's updated his style:

> Look at the rhododendrons! They don't give a toss
> about the funding cuts, the polar bears. They do
> their own thing. Throw your keys into that hedge,
> ignore the cameras. Be your own true kicking self.

Douglas Houston's *Beyond the playing fields: New and Selected Poems, 1980-2010* was published by Shoestring Press in 2010.

Border Stories

SARAH WARDLE

Liz Lochhead, *A Choosing: Selected Poems*,
Polygon, £9.99, ISBN 9781846972072;
James Berry, *A Story I Am In: Selected Poems*, Bloodaxe,
£10.95, ISBN 9781852249175;
Christopher Reid, *Selected Poems*, Faber, £14.99, ISBN 9780571273270

A Choosing contains a selection of Liz Lochhead's poetry from her first book in 1972 to her appointment as Makar of Scotland in 2011. Her poetry is rich, mature and as alluringly complex as a single malt, full of strong street speech and gentle lyric strains. She was a trailblazer for liberated women's poetry and has influenced younger poets from all over, as well as those within her country, like Jackie Kay and Kathleen Jamie. These poems are not arranged chronologically but in interesting pairings, where one offsets another. The title echoes one of her best-loved poems, 'The Choosing', which chronicles the divergence of two girls' paths in life, the poet and her equally clever, junior-school friend whose reactionary father does not approve of women's education: "I think of those prizes that were ours for the taking / and wonder when the choices got made / we don't remember making". Paired with this is 'Kidspoem / Bairnsang', a poem about a child's first day at school alternating between Scots and RP English, which highlights the values of hometown dialects as much as 'The Choosing' valued traditional education.

'What the Pool Said, On Midsummer's Day', an enticingly sensual, even raunchy, poem, is in the voice of a pool to a man she invites to her, like a lover. 'Last Supper' is similarly strong and active, not passive, marking the end of a relationship with a commemorative feast with the girls, yet aware that "somebody would get hungry / and go hunting again".

'View of Scotland / Love Poem' is representative of both her realism and her romantic streak: "So there's a bottle of sickly liqueur / among the booze in the alcove, / golden crusts on steak pies / like quilts on a double bed". Realism balanced by tenderness pervades other poems, such as 'Social History', about "The sex my mother could've had / but didn't", and 'For My Grandmother Knitting', a tribute to her grandmother's work as fisher-girl, miner's wife, mother, grandmother, arthritic hands still working to the last. These are poems to stir and make us think, of the kind she describes in 'Poets Need Not', which come "as leaves do", poetry "insisting it be heard and seen".

A Story I Am In, the title James Berry has given his selection, draws attention to how he is but one among a brotherhood, society, history. Here are poems of struggle and injustice, energy and spirit. 'Beginning in a City, 1948' vividly tells of his arrival as an economic migrant in London, where "war-tired people moved slowly" with "Grimy bundles [...] bags were pets", how he "searched without knowing [...] walked without map, without knowledge / from Victoria to Brixton", where a "brodda" helped him with advice for the "jus-come". He chronicles the ignorance and prejudice he meets from white adults and children, and the British police. In 'Travelling As We Are', he recounts his anger as he journeys to work on the tube in the Fifties, "British among Britons", and overhears a boy from the American South asking, "But this is Europe, Mummy. How come / niggers live here too?" In 'White Child Meets Black Man', a small girl asks, "Mummy is his tummy black?" 'On an Afternoon Train from Purley to Victoria, 1955' sees Berry respond to a pleasant but ignorant young Quaker woman who asked, "What part of Africa is Jamaica?" by saying "Where Ireland is near Lapland", before generously observing "So sincere she was beautiful". 'In-a Brixtan Markit' is a fine slow-motion replay of how he checked his emotions when stopped and searched by a police officer who had picked on him: "'Tony,' I say, 'hol on. Hol on, / Tony. Dohn shove [...] Battn down.' An, man, Tony win."

'Confession' is an important poem, written in the voice of a girl turning seventeen, whose coming of age and awareness enables her to see through social conditioning. She used to have a "condition" in which she believed her mother's words that "black people were cursed". Now she sees "other people in struggle" too. 'In Our Year 1941 My Letter to You Mother Africa' transmits the ambivalence Berry felt towards his ancestral homeland: "you sold my ancestors / labelled, not for human rights", and describes how he set his sights further afield than his father: "I want a university in me [...] I refuse to be Estate 'chop-bush' man / and a poverty path scarecrow". 'Reasons for Leaving Jamaica' is a touching poem about how hardship motivated characters like Berry to sail for Britain; the dialect, as in so many of the poems, is an example of the culture he brought with him, as is the wisdom of 'Folk Proverbs Found Poems', which includes the advice, "Is better to walk for nothing / than sit down for so-so".

Christopher Reid's *Selected Poems* sees him move from the playfulness of his early Martian metaphors to the haunting sorrow of *A Scattering*, while his gifts for apt expression and poetic truth, which won him the Costa Prize, are evident throughout. In the early poem, 'H. Vernon', a butcher displays pigs with ears like cherubs' wings and takes delivery of carcasses whose flanks are "strung with ribs like enormous harps", as if these wretched animals had souls. Another early poem, 'At the Wrong Door', foreshadows the proximity to absence of *A Scattering*; but here it is merely a spatial separation from his wife, not one of death: "I have missed you by a minute [...] your / absence palpable in the misty, / trickling, inexorcisable ghost / that occupies the whole mirror".

Katerina Brac seems a project more of ventriloquism than satire. 'What the Uneducated Woman Told Me' does not mock, but juxtaposes the particular and local with general wisdom about old age and widowhood. Similarly, 'Consulting the Oracle' is at once about particular detail and primary evidence and at the same time all visits to the elderly, where you jab the lift button, "jogging its memory". 'Memres of Alfred Stoker' continues his exploration of monologue and translation, as well as his engagement with religion, seen in other poems such as 'From Information Received' with its official, imperial tone: "I don't believe / we need fear this cult".

Reid is the kindly vicar or housemaster of contemporary English poetry and delights in the well-chosen word, often intellectual, whimsical or wry. So in 'By the By' the vocabulary is phrased "the whole enterprise rested / on his glorious disdain / for so-called alphabetical order"; in 'Fly' "a gap of air / waits, but this has / not yet been vouchsafed to the fly". He writes with verve and panache. 'Bollockshire' is a brilliant evocation of middle England – its landscape, economy, legends – which makes one glad to live in either a deep rural, or metropolitan, environment. *Mr Mouth* is full of imaginative, mythic, witty riffs on his theme.

The title poem of his award-winning collection of elegies pictures a wildlife documentary to which he profoundly relates: elephants scattering a herd member's bones in mourning: "Elephants puzzling out / the anagram of their own anatomy, / elephants at their abstracted lamentations". In deeply touching poems he writes out the worst weight of his grief, expressing emotion, as in 'Late', with apparently casual ease: "it was already too late / and she'd wisped clean away". By the closing poem, 'Afterlife', he can move on: "I had work to do, too".

Sarah Wardle's most recent collection is *A Knowable World* (Bloodaxe).

Deep Pollen

ERIK MARTINY

Peter Redgrove, *Collected Poems*, Cape, £25, ISBN 9780224090278;
Neil Roberts, *A Lucid Dreamer: The Life of Peter Redgrove*,
Cape, £30, ISBN 9780224090292

"This is no book; who touches this, touches a man" – so Walt Whitman famously remarked about his own collected poems. Jonathan Cape's joint release of Peter Redgrove's first *Collected Poems* alongside Neil Roberts's biography certainly allows the reader to place a finger on the uniambic pulse of this flamboyantly original poet. Roberts, one of the foremost English critics, offers many an insightful glimpse into both the outer and the inner man who suffers, the one that T.S. Eliot felt should always remain concealed. Although some of Redgrove's poems are autobiographical, he tended for the most part to eschew the minutiae of the man-about-town in favour of natural miracles and the ghost in the machine.

It is, for instance, possible to read Redgrove's final collections, put together when he was both physically and mentally crippled by Parkinson's and other illnesses, without detecting a hint of speedily approaching finitude or declining power. At most, a "lady doctor" will make an appearance in an otherworldly coat to allay anxiety and sex the cherry of a poem. Ignoring pain and suffering, keeping defeatism at bay, transmuting negativity into lexical magic, is what Redgrove's poetry is all about.

His work is so intent on celebration that he has been taxed with being apolitical. Conjuring up nature's cathedrals out of trees and waterfalls has sometimes led him down the risky politically incorrect path: one of his early poems, 'The Sermon', goes as far as to locate God in the explosion of an atom bomb. Admittedly, the speaker of the poem is a priest, but there is no real attempt to genuinely dissociate the author from the numinously eloquent narrator, nor to demarcate the lyric from the dramatic monologue. This is not to say that Redgrove was in favour of nuclear weapons, or that he would blithely extol poverty the way Whitman did.

Roberts's account of Redgrove's life, unfortunately, does not go into his attitudes to topical issues, but the strengths of his biography are manifold. Roberts's extensive research into archived material, coupled to his long-standing friendship with the poet and his widow, Penelope Shuttle, make this a bracing account of the life, even for those who have detailed knowledge of the work.

The early chapters of the biography offer pupil-dilating insights into Redgrove's relationship to his parents, as well as an elaboration of his unusual erotic experiments which Roberts convincingly suggests became the fundamental wellspring of his poetry.

Redgrove's early involvement with science at Cambridge University and later estrangement from that discipline is interestingly counterpointed by Roberts with the contemporaneous discovery of the structure of DNA at Cambridge, an exciting line of research which might have fuelled Redgrove's lagging interest in pure science. As was the case with Erasmus Darwin before him, the natural sciences continued to inform Redgrove's poetry. Roberts cites Redgrove as having said that "people who called him a surrealist had never looked through a microscope". This is of course a partially misleading dismissal as Redgrove's poetry often has recourse to elaborately contrived surreal defamiliarisation or incongruous juxtaposition.

There are some engrossing passages in Roberts's biography on Redgrove's friendship and rivalry with such key figures as Ted Hughes, D. M. Thomas and Angela Carter, whose novels Redgrove mistakenly hoped would create a space for his own novelistic pursuits in the genre of magic realism. In the end, although there are other factors involved, one might say that Redgrove's relative lack of popularity was caused by his refusal to compose mostly tidy poems that focus on a single subject as Hughes's often did, or novels with a strong central storyline, which is what Carter's novels possessed, despite their oneiric atmosphere. Redgrove's experimental, teeming imagination often carried his work in multiple directions within the same work: one way of describing it would be to say that as well as being what Kathleen Raine called "a waterfall in full spate", the air around it is also humming with pollen, particles of God and gorgeously jetting dragonflies.

Roberts's account of Redgrove's relationship to the eccentric Jungian disciple John Layard is particularly revealing and thorough, occasionally prompting the reader to raise an eyebrow. We learn, for instance, that Layard invited Redgrove to touch his penis as part of his therapy, an experience that inspired the following semi-comic surreal line: "I felt his little soft penis and stroked it: his whole skin was penis-like, soft as a gazelle's nose".

There are moments when the biography seems to contradict the collected poems: although Roberts does not deny Redgrove's attachment to his children, he makes him out to be a rather distant, inadequate father whose interest in writing far surpassed his desire for connection with his offspring. Poems such as 'Bedtime Story For My Son' or 'The Visible Baby' seem to tell a different story. His children were a steady source of inspiration to him: the figure of the baby that recurs is not just an avatar of the filius philosophorum of bygone alchemists, and those poems that evoke them often express a father's intensely tender bond in terms that are imaginatively stirring. Witness this x-ray visioned scientist-sonneteer's love-inspired blazon for a child:

> There are his teeth in his transparent gums like a budding hawthorn
> > twig,
>
> His eyes like open poppies follow the light,
> His tongue is like a crest of his thumping blood,
> His heart like two squirrels one scarlet, one purple
> Mating in the canopy of a blood-tree;
>
> His spine like a necklace, all silvery-strung with cartilages,
> His handbones like a working-party of white insects,
> His nerves like a tree of ice with sunlight shooting through it,
>
> What a closed book bound in wrinkled illustrations his father is to him!

Erik Martiny teaches literature and film studies in the Paris region. He has just edited *A Companion to Poetic Genre* for Wiley-Blackwell.

Order In Disorder

RACHEL REDFORD

Andrew Greig, *As Though We Were Flying*, Bloodaxe,
£8.95, ISBN 9781852249168;
Philip Gross, *Deep Field*, Bloodaxe, £8.95. ISBN 9781852249199;
Peter Scupham, *Borrowed Landscapes*, Carcanet, £9.95. ISBN 9781847770806;
Anthony Caleshu, *Of Whales in print, in paint, in sea, in stars, in coin, in house, in margins*, Salt, £9.99 ISBN 9781844715022;
Chris Kinsey, *Swarf*, Smokestack Books, £7.95. ISBN 9780956417527

*A*s *Though We Were Flying* is the Scottish poet Andrew Greig's tenth book of poetry, containing what his mentor Norman MacCaig called "honey and salt" and what Greig himself calls "praises and elegies for what has been and is". Scotland is Greig's *locus*, where he "comes home / to roost". Anstruther, where he grew up in the early sixties with its "dying shops" selling vests and elastic, is presented through crisp, concise images with "what has been" seen further in Anstruther's tidal swimming pool, once filled with "the gift of tides" and now reduced to slimy weeds and slabs. Fishermen no longer make a living: old Alex Watson sat "uncomplaining as cancer ate him, / eyebrows like spray, quiet as haar", as though being absorbed back into the "haar", the almost onomatopoeic Scots word for sea-mist in which you can hear its white breath. The Scots language scattered throughout these poems contributes to their lean precision and gives them both muscle and music.

Memory – sharp, poignant and reflective – is the core of Greig's work. Young Eck Hutchinson, drowned while lobster fishing, is forever nineteen years old, "snagged on those skerries". Now in "late middle years", Greig muses with piercing accuracy that it is "as though memory were a frozen loch / bearing us up where we can never / be again". Combining both elegy and "praise for what is", he recalls the hands of his surgeon father "that now are ash", and feels him "lighting up the branching pathways" as he sits at his desk "working these words". This "working" results in images that infuse the ordinary with a further dimension, while the skill of Greig the musician is reflected in the balanced phrasing and chiming, lilting sounds.

The questioning of human existence in Philip Gross's *Deep Field* echoes the theme of his collection *The Water Table*, which won the T.S. Eliot Prize in 2009. The word "space" recurs in this new collection in which he explores the gradual loss of speech experienced by his elderly father. *The Deep Field* image taken by the Hubble space telescope, which revealed thousands of the youngest and most distant galaxies, inspires Gross's analogies and his questing. "With time a few / stray photons may come straggling in / from space": could this aphasia be not an end, but a beginning yet unknown? Gross's father, an Estonian refugee, once had five languages and "made blankness into words" as he solved Ximenes's crosswords. Now his words are blankness. Gross searches the space into which language has vanished, where something – perhaps memories – must surely still be:

> if I   could catch   the silence there
> take space   take any space   that's deep enough
>   between   the language   and the atrophy
> the MRI   reveals   the mis-
>   placed   memories   the glare
> of history   still we   may be there may-
>   be we   may   be

The spaces between words on the page reflect the gaps in "the weft" of his father's neurons, while their careful alignment shows Gross striving to find sense in senselessness, order in disorder.

Gross's frames of reference are elemental: the sea, wind, emptiness. Childhood memories of the sea merge into metaphors of separation with Gross on one shore and his father "adrift on the vowel stream" on another, his words "washed up at the tideline". In an echo of his father's flight from Estonia long ago, he has once more become a foreigner in that "gone place", displaced, "away on the wind". These poems are Gross's intellectual and moving search for a way across the chasm made by loss of language.

Peter Scupham is now approaching eighty and *Borrowed Landscapes* is his first publication since *Collected Poems* in 2003. In these poems memories and a sense of loss are as omnipresent as water and wind. Gulls mew "in animal grief for the quick and the dead"; among the "spilt brains of bladderwrack" and the "wraiths of sea mist" on the estuary, he sees "the outstretched hands you long ago let slip". Scupham's tight verse forms and metre dispel melancholy and suggest controlled, analysed emotion.

In the sequence *A Civil War* Scupham uses family archives to explore the wartime experiences of his German father-in-law, a distinguished academic, who served with British forces during the First World War. In a series of poems entitled *Playtime in a Cold City*, he relives his Cambridge undergraduate years punctuated by reservist training in the mid 1950s. His world of the "obligatory" pipe and Millets duffle coat, punting and being "drunk on Nescafé and buttered sausages" is tempered by memory and threat of war. His father's undergraduate days "*entre deux guerres*"coexist with his own as, under Leavis, he reassembles dismantled poems "like Bren guns", aware of the chill as "Cold War glaciers / grow even colder" and"Soviet tanks grind into Budapest".

The natural world is jagged with harsh elements. Even the rooks "tear pieces from the sky" and scarecrows recall haunting imagery of war: "over wool-gathering / nail and thorn / nightmares hung / on the old barbed wire. / Monstrous crows / quarrel over eyes." Unalloyed comfort is found only, it seems, in the "throbbing chest" of his fondled cat.

Chris Kinsey's world in *Swarf* is that of "maisonettes and out-houses", conversations heard at the back of the bus, boys doing wheelies. Her skill is to reveal the heart of a "trapped wren" in ordinary, marginalised people: carers, hospital patients, the housebound; even"sad bastard Colin", turned on by "fucking fish", is given a witty colloquial voice. Glimpses of her childhood are vivid: the excitement of chemistry and boxing; her welder father "coming home deaf and ragged, / swarf in his soles". Kinsey is at her best, however, with nature. Here the language is more striking, the content less anecdotal. A kingfisher "falters / on a spillage of turquoise"; "spillage" encapsulates that sudden flash of iridescence. Another striking visual metaphor captures the flight of a goose, "unpicking the seam where the weather fronts merge".

Anthony Caleshu left America in 1997 and now teaches at the University of Plymouth. *Of Whales* shows him caught in Herman Melville's mythic noose. He is steeped in *Moby Dick*, Melville's letters, references and marginalia, and associated literature, quotations from which preface the poems. Interpreted and re-imagined, the fruits of his research are in abundance as Caleshu shape-changes into adventurer, crew member, navigator, or captain of the whaling ship. Entwined with these reworkings is the "you" addressed in some poems: the baby son the poet soothes at night, "That wonderfullest thing which is ever unmentionable... / I take stock of you like a second heart, a third lung" ('Wonderfullest Thing'). Caleshu combines Melville's words with his own here, and the meshing of themes is effective and moving. Elsewhere the mix is mired in indulgent reference and cross-reference. Caleshu displays adventurous linguistic vigour and also playful alliteration – "We'd been wooing whaleslike women once wooed us"– but meaning for the reader is often sacrificed in the heat of experiment.

Rachel Redford is a writer and reviewer with a special interest in poetry.

Light And Grace

JEM POSTER

Maitreyabandhu, *The Bond*, Smith/Doorstop, £5, ISBN 9781906613488;
Esther Morgan, *Grace*, Bloodaxe, £8.95, ISBN 9781852249182;
Julian Turner, *Planet-Struck*, Anvil Press, £8.95, ISBN 9780856464355;
Kwame Dawes, *Wheels*, Peepal Tree Press, $19.95, ISBN 9781845231422

An ordained member of the Triratna Buddhist Order and a poet and teacher of some distinction, Maitreyabandhu has spoken of the connection between his artistic and his spiritual vocations. Quoting Auden – "The primary function of poetry, as of all the arts, is to make us more aware of ourselves and the world around us" – he noted in a 2009 *Guardian* interview that poetry had become "another strand of my spiritual practice". The poems in this slim but satisfying pamphlet are certainly characterised by a quiet lucidity of vision; and if the poet's contemplative gaze seems more strongly focused on past events than on the present moment generally recommended in Buddhist meditative practice, this can be taken to imply a complication rather than a contradiction.

It's the poet's own past that preoccupies him, in particular the events of his childhood and youth. Poems such as 'The Chest of Drawers' and 'Copper Wire' lovingly recreate a world of small pleasures, discoveries and terrors: a polish tin given to the child to hold while his mother gets on with the ironing, a discarded strand of wire wrestled from the earth by a father who lets nothing go to waste, the nightmares not quite held at bay by maternal love. Even where adolescent sexuality enters the frame, the vision itself remains essentially childlike, though a more knowing adult perspective is implied in a recurrent questioning of the authenticity of memory.

The ordinariness of the remembered events doesn't preclude a sense of mystery, and in one poem, 'The Small Boy and the Mouse', the childhood experience is an overtly visionary one. The poem concludes with an image of all-encompassing light and the suggestion that the everyday world – or the boy's perception of it – has been subtly but importantly transformed by what he has seen or imagined: "He opened his eyes. All the furniture / looked strange, as if someone had rearranged it."

The lines find echoes in Esther Morgan's 'Among Women', in which the

Virgin Mary (or some version of her) experiences the Annunciation in similar terms, as a transfiguration of the ordinary:

> One evening I came back home
> and everything was just as I'd left it –
> except the bowls gleamed with a new knowledge

The visionary gleam is picked up and amplified by poem after poem in Morgan's superb new collection. It's there in the "saintly dazzle" of a sheet hung out to dry, or a door handle that "gleams / like the foot of an icon / rubbed into brightness"; or again, with an only marginally more secular slant, in the "galaxies of light blazing / in the mirror's bevelled edge" and a suite of rooms "tidal / with light".

Morgan's passion for light is also a yearning for space and air, for an uncluttered and ethereal existence. "I want to come back as sunlight," she writes in 'Last Summer': "to steal over everything I own / with the warmth of skin / that isn't there." It's an impulse implicit in the collection's tendency to locate its actors at the edge of things, often with a suggestion of the potential for release into a wider world. Windows figure significantly: a woman whose childhood home backed on to open countryside now stands at the kitchen window looking out over "dawning fields"; a voice invokes a dream "of waking in a room with a wide open window, / the air clear and ringing after night rain"; and a woman hearing lark-song as she shakes her duster from an upstairs window experiences an airy epiphany – a sense of "leaning into a blue / which seemed, like the spiralling arias, / to carry on forever."

If air is the dominant element in *Grace*, Julian Turner's *Planet-Struck* is ruled by earth and water. Turner's topographies are often specific to his home in the Yorkshire Dales and the poems convey a powerful sense of physical engagement with the landscapes they describe. Thorns pluck at the speaker's coat, sleet stings his face; he climbs a hillside "in drumming rain when the ground goes liquid / and pours between the roots of ash". When, in 'The Yoredale Beds', he places his ear against the turf "to hear my heart / sound underground", the fusion or confusion of self and landscape seems absolutely appropriate.

Turner has an archaeologist's eye for the marks left on the land by vanished societies and civilisations – rings and standing stones, the turfed mound of a burial site, the contours of a Bronze Age village. These are not, for him, objects of merely scientific interest, but a means of calling up the ghosts of the land's lost inhabitants – the questionable shades of:

drovers or husbandmen
walking along the old roads
in sunken lanes below
the surface of the present world.

These are solid and serious poems, but not entirely skilful ones. The precise points at which their knotty muscularity becomes a form of awkwardness may be debatable, but it is certainly the case that the collection is technically uneven: clumsy phrasing mars a number of the poems, and Turner's sense of rhythm and cadence sometimes seems to desert him. Even so, there's a great deal here to admire and enjoy.

Kwame Dawes's output over the past twenty years has been prodigious – novels, plays, essays, anthologies and more than a dozen volumes of poetry – and his extraordinary energy informs this new collection at every level. The imaginative reach of the poems is immense: they offer us visions of Old Testament landscapes or pitch us into the turmoil of a slave revolt in eighteenth century South Carolina; they follow Haile Selassie from Ethiopia into exile in 1930s Bath or propel us through the hot, violent streets of contemporary Kingston. As we travel with him, Dawes gives voice and substance to a range of characters, most notably, in a monumental seventy-page sequence, the HIV-infected and the dispossessed of Port au Prince in the aftermath of the Haitian earthquake of 2010.

Many of the voices are the voices of prophecy (the wheels of the collection's title are those of Ezekiel's vision) and their message is bleak: "All around us / the whisper is of 'Last Days', the coming / of the end, and the tyranny of present danger." Images of death and destruction proliferate: fruit rots on city stalls, murdered bodies are scattered among broken incense bowls, a man and woman make love "beside the rotting carcases of beached / dolphins". The effect might have been dispiriting, but it isn't – or, at least, not entirely so. Somewhere beyond the darkness and dissolution lies another vision: "the light of bones, a flaming, the grace / of new dawns at the breaking of old graves."

Jem Poster is a poet and novelist; he holds the Chair of Creative Writing at Aberystwyth University.

Dorothy Sargent Rosenberg Annual Poetry Prizes, 2012

PRIZE WINNERS FOR OUR 2011 COMPETITION, ANNOUNCED FEBRUARY 5, 2012

$10,000 PRIZES to Jeremy Bass and James Crews

$7,500 PRIZES to Jenny George, Brittany Perham and Christine Poreba

$5,000 prizes to Josh Booton, Traci Brimhall, Michelle Y. Burke, Kai Carlson-Wee, Jeannine Hall Gailey, Brieghan Gardner, Emily Rosko and Eleanor Stanford

$2,500 prizes to Douglas Basford, Holly Virginia Clark, Katy Didden, Maia Evrona, Jules Gibbs, Amy Greacen, Brenna W. Lemieux, Rebecca Lindenberg, John Newsham, Rachel Richardson, Joshua Rivkin, Will Schutt, Ali Shapiro, Matthew Thorburn, Rhett Iseman Trull and Mark Wagenaar

$1,000 prizes to Lauren K. Alleyne, Brian Brodeur, James Everett, Maria Hummel, Henry Kearney IV, Deirdre Lockwood, Éireann Lorsung, Ariana Nadia Nash, Christian Teresi and Chelsea Wagenaar

There were also seventeen Honorable Mentions at $250 each

THANK YOU TO EVERYONE WHO ENTERED AND CONGRATULATIONS TO OUR WINNERS

WE NOW HAPPILY ANNOUNCE OUR

2012 Competition

Prizes ranging from $1,000 up to as much as $25,000 will be awarded for the finest lyric poems celebrating the human spirit. The contest is open to all writers, published or unpublished, who will be under the age of 40 on November 6, 2012. Entries must be postmarked on or before the third Saturday in October (October 20, 2012). Only previously unpublished poems are eligible for prizes. Names of prize winners will be published on our website on February 5, 2013, together with a selection of the winning poems. Please visit our website www.DorothyPrizes.org for further information and to read poems by previous winners.

CHECKLIST OF CONTEST GUIDELINES

- Entries must be postmarked on or before October 20, 2012.
- Past winners may re-enter until their prizes total in excess of $25,000.
- All entrants must be under the age of 40 on November 6, 2012.
- Submissions must be original, previously unpublished, and in English: no translations, please.
- Each entrant may submit one to three separate poems.
- Only one of the poems may be more than thirty lines in length.
- Each poem must be printed on a separate sheet.
- Submit two copies of each entry with your name, address, phone number and email address clearly marked on each page of one copy only.
- Include an index card with your name, address, phone number and email address and the titles of each of your submitted poems.
- Include a $10 entry fee payable to the Dorothy Sargent Rosenberg Memorial Fund. (This fee is not required for entrants resident outside the USA.)
- Poems will not be returned. Include a stamped addressed envelope if you wish us to acknowledge receipt of your entry.

MAIL ENTRIES TO: Dorothy Sargent Rosenberg Poetry Prizes, PO Box 2306, Orinda, California 94563, USA